Fodor's POCKET

san francisco

fourteenth edition

Excerpted from *Fodor's California*

fodor's travel publications
new york • toronto • london • sydney • auckland
www.fodors.com

contents

maps

on the road
with Fodor's

THE MORE YOU KNOW BEFORE YOU GO, the better your trip will be.
San Francisco's most fascinating small museum or best
Vietnamese noodle house could be just around the corner from
your hotel, but if you don't know it's there, it might as well be
across the globe. That's where this guidebook and our Web site,
Fodors.com, come in. Our editors work hard to give you useful,
on-target information. Their efforts begin with finding the best
contributors—people with good judgment and broad travel
experience—the people you'd poll for tips yourself if you knew
them.

Don't Forget to Write

Your experiences—positive and negative—matter to us. If we
have missed or misstated something, we want to hear about it.
We follow up on all suggestions. Contact the California editor at
editors@fodors.com or c/o Fodor's, 280 Park Avenue, New York,
NY 10017. And have a fabulous trip!

Karen Cure

Karen Cure
Editorial Director

the bay area

San Pablo Bay

San Rafael

Richmond–San Rafael Bridge

Richmond

Martinez

John Muir National Historic Site

Briones Regional Park

El Cerrito

Tilden Regional Park

Mt. Tamalpais State Park

Muir Woods

Mill Valley

Tiburon

Angel I.

Berkeley

Marin City

Golden Gate Nat'l. Recreation Area

Sausalito

Treasure I.

SF–Oakland Bay Br.

Lake Merritt

Redwood Regional Park

Golden Gate Bridge

TO PT. REYES

SAN FRANCISCO

Yerba Buena I.

Oakland

Daly City

Oakland International Airport

San Leandro

Pacifica

San Francisco International Airport

Hayward Regional Shoreline

Hayward

San Francisco Bay

Coyote Pt. Nature Museum

Burlingame

San Mateo

San Mateo Br.

Montara

Crystal Springs Reservoir

Belmont

Dumbarton Br.

Half Moon Bay

Redwood City

Palo Alto

Baylands Nature Interpretive Center

Filoli

Woodside

Stanford University

N

PACIFIC OCEAN

10 miles

15 km

san francisco

PACIFIC OCEAN

Golden Gate Bridge
Fort Point
101

Golden Gate
National
Recreation
Area

The Presidio

Palace
of the
Legion
of Honor

Baker
Beach

Land's
End

Phelan
Beach

Lake St.

Lincoln
Park

Clement St.

SEACLIFF

Park Presidio Blvd.

8th Ave.

Arguello Blvd.

Point
Lobos

Geary Blvd.

34th Ave.

25th Ave.

19th Ave.

Balboa St.

Turk

Seal
Rocks

Cliff
House

43rd Ave.

RICHMOND

Fulton St.

Golden Gate Park

Slow
Lake

GOLDEN

Beach
Chalet

Kennedy Dr.

Middle Dr.

7th Ave.

Funston Ave.

Lincoln Way

Judah St.

GATE

28th Ave.

Lawton St.

1

Noriega St.

19th Ave.

Ortega St.

NATIONAL

41st Ave.

Sunset Blvd.

SUNSET

Quintara St.

14th Ave.

Dewey Blvd.

Clarendon

Taraval St.

McCoppin
Square

Vicente St.

Larsen
Park

Portola

Dr.

Yerba Buena Ave.

M
Davi

Stern Grove

RECREATION

San Francisco
Zoo

Sloat Blvd.

STONESTOWN

Monterey

Blvd.

Miramar

Ocean

Junipero Serra Blvd.

Harding
Park

San Francisco
State Univ.

Holloway Ave.

mouth Ave.

Skyline Blvd.

Lake Merced

Lake Merced Blvd.

Font Blvd.

Garfield St.

AREA

Fort
Funston

0   1 mile
0   1 km

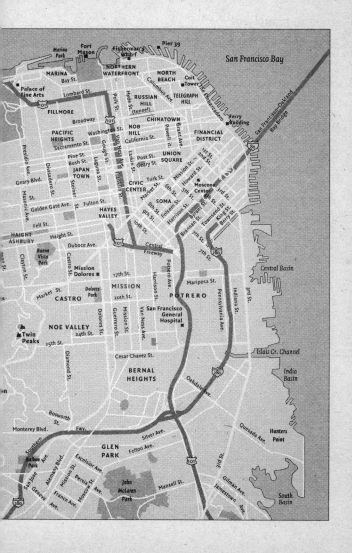

san francisco

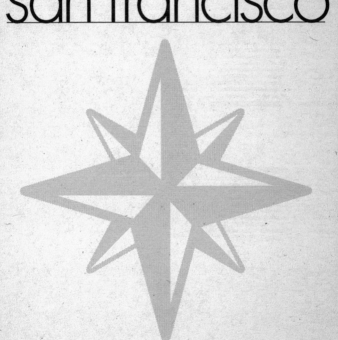

In This Chapter

introducing
san francisco

THAT VISITORS WILL ENVY SAN FRANCISCANS is a given—at least, so say Bay Area residents, who tend to pity anyone who did not have the foresight to settle here. Their self-satisfaction may surprise some, considering how the city has been battered by fires and earthquakes from the 1840s onward, most notably in the 1906 conflagration and again in 1989, when the Loma Prieta earthquake rocked the city's foundations and caused serious damage to the Marina District as well as to numerous local freeways. Since its earliest days San Francisco has been a phoenix, the mythical bird that periodically dies in flame to be reborn in greater grandeur.

Its latest rebirth has occurred in SoMa, the neighborhood south of Market Street, where the Yerba Buena Gardens development has taken shape with the world-class SFMOMA (San Francisco Museum of Modern Art) at its heart—transforming a formerly seedy neighborhood into a magnet of culture. As a peninsula city, surrounded on three sides by water, San Francisco grows from the inside out. Its blighted areas are improved, not abandoned. The museum development's instant success—measured by a huge influx of residents, suburban commuters, and international visitors—perfectly exemplifies this tradition.

San Francisco has long been a bastion of what it likes to refer to as "progressive politics." The Sierra Club, founded here in 1892 by John Muir, has its national headquarters on Polk Street. The turn-of-the-20th-century "yellow journalism" of William

Randolph Hearst's *San Francisco Examiner* gave way to such leftist publications as *Mother Jones* magazine and today's left-of-center weekly newspapers.

Loose, tolerant, and even licentious are words that are used to describe San Francisco. Bohemian communities thrive here. As early as the 1860s the Barbary Coast—a collection of taverns, whorehouses, and gambling joints along Pacific Avenue close to the waterfront—was famous, or infamous. North Beach, the city's Little Italy, became the home of the Beat movement in the 1950s (Herb Caen, the city's best-known columnist, coined the term beatnik). Lawrence Ferlinghetti's City Lights, a bookstore and publishing house that still stands on Columbus Avenue, brought out, among other titles, Allen Ginsberg's *Howl* and *Kaddish*.

In the '60s the Free Speech Movement began at the University of California at Berkeley, and Stanford's David Harris, who went to prison for defying the draft, numbered among the nation's most famous student leaders. In October 1965 Allen Ginsberg introduced the term *flower power*, and the Haight-Ashbury district became synonymous with hippiedom, giving rise to such legendary bands as Jefferson Airplane and the Grateful Dead. Thirty years later the Haight's history and its name still draw neo-hippies, as well as new wavers with black lips and blue hair. Transients make panhandling one of Haight Street's major business activities, and the potential for crime and violence after dark has turned many of the liberal residents into unlikely law-and-order advocates. Still, most remain committed to keeping the Haight the Haight.

Southwest of the Haight is the onetime Irish neighborhood known as the Castro, which during the 1970s became identified with gay and lesbian liberation. Castro Street is dominated by the elaborate Castro Theatre, a 1922 vision in Spanish baroque style, which presents first-run art and independent films with occasional revivals of Hollywood film classics. The Castro is an effervescent neighborhood, and—as housing everywhere has become more scarce—an increasingly mixed one. At the same time, gays, like Asians, are moving out of the ghetto and into neighborhoods all around the city.

In terms of both geography and culture, San Francisco is about as close as you can get to Asia in the continental United States. The first great wave of Chinese immigrants came as railroad laborers. Chinese workers quickly became the target of race hatred and discriminatory laws. Chinatown began when the Chinese moved into old buildings that white businesses seeking more fashionable locations had abandoned. It is still a fascinating place to wander and a good bet for late-night food, but it's not the whole story by any means. The Asian community reaches into every San Francisco neighborhood and particularly into the Sunset and Richmond districts, west toward the ocean. San Francisco also has its Japantown, with the Japan Center complex and a handful of shops and restaurants. Establishing themselves over the decades, today Asian Americans are at the highest levels of the city's elected and appointed government and in leadership positions in San Francisco's professional communities.

Geographically, San Francisco is the thumbnail on a 40-mi thumb of land, the San Francisco Peninsula, which stretches northward between the Pacific Ocean and San Francisco Bay. Hemmed in on three sides by water, its land area (less than 50 square mi) is relatively small. The population, at about 750,000, is small, too. Technically speaking, it's only California's fourth-largest city, but that statistic is misleading: The Bay Area, extending from the bedroom communities north of Oakland and Berkeley south through the peninsula and the San Jose area, is really one continuous megacity, with San Francisco at its heart.

Victorian architecture is as integral to the city as fog and cable cars. Bay-windowed, ornately decorated Victorian houses—the ahistorical, multicolor paint jobs that have become popular make them seem even more ornate—are the city's most distinguishing architectural feature. They date mainly from the latter part of Queen Victoria's reign, 1870 to the turn of the 20th century. In those three decades San Francisco more than doubled in population (from 150,000 to 342,000); the transcontinental railway, linking the once-isolated western capital to the East, had been completed in 1869. That may explain the exuberant confidence of the architecture.

Another measure of the city's exuberance is its many festivals and celebrations. The Lesbian, Gay, Bisexual, and Transgendered Pride Parade and Celebration held each June, vies with the Chinese New Year's Parade, an annual February event, as the city's most elaborate. They both get competition from Japantown's Cherry Blossom Festival, in April; the Columbus Day and St. Patrick's Day parades; Carnaval, held in the Hispanic Mission District in May; and the May Day march, a labor celebration in a labor town. The mix of ethnic, economic, social, and sexual groups can be bewildering, but the city's residents—whatever their origin—face it with aplomb and even gratitude. Nearly everyone smiles on the fortunate day they arrived on this windy, foggy patch of peninsula.

QUICK TOURS

TOUR ONE

Start your day downtown at **UNION SQUARE**. Explore tiny Maiden Lane (east of the square) before walking north on Grant Avenue through the **CHINATOWN** gate. From Chinatown continue into **NORTH BEACH**; walking north on Columbus Avenue or Grant Avenue you'll pass any number of San Francisco landmarks from the Beat era. From Washington Square in North Beach, walk or take Muni Bus 39 to **COIT TOWER** atop Telegraph Hill for a fabulous view of the entire bay.

TOUR TWO

Make reservations for a **BOAT RIDE TO ALCATRAZ** (call at least a week in advance during the summer); boats leave from the Fisherman's Wharf area. If you have time after the boat ride, walk west along Beach Street to Hyde Street, where you can either take a ride on the **POWELL-HYDE CABLE CAR** or explore the historic vessels anchored at the **HYDE STREET PIER**.

TOUR THREE

Explore the eastern half of **GOLDEN GATE PARK.** Begin at the **CONSERVATORY OF FLOWERS** and walk west on John F. Kennedy Drive to Tea Garden Drive. Stop into the **M. H. DE YOUNG MUSEUM,** which has a very fine collection of American art. The **ASIAN ART MUSEUM** is part of the de Young complex. After visiting the museums, stop at the **JAPANESE TEA GARDEN,** adjacent to the Asian Art Museum, for a soothing cup of tea. If you've still got time, head south across the Music Concourse to the **CALIFORNIA ACADEMY OF SCIENCES**.

TOUR FOUR

Begin South of Market (**SOMA**) at **YERBA BUENA GARDENS.** Across the street is the **SAN FRANCISCO MUSEUM OF CONTEMPORARY ART.** From the museum walk up 3rd Street to Market Street and then walk west on Market to the **CABLE-CAR TERMINUS** at Powell Street, where you can catch either the Powell-Hyde or the Powell-Mason cable car to **NOB HILL.** If you walk to Nob Hill, it's about eight blocks, four of which are fairly steep. At the intersection of Powell and California streets walk west one block on California Street. After exploring Nob Hill, slip into the **TONGA ROOM** at the Fairmount Hotel for a tropical cocktail (if it's earlier than 5 PM, head across California Street to the **TOP OF THE MARK** at Mark Hopkins Inter-Continental Hotel).

In This Chapter

Revised by Denise M. Leto

here and there

SAN FRANCISCO IS A RELATIVELY SMALL CITY. About 750,000 residents live on a 46½-square-mi tip of land between San Francisco Bay and the Pacific Ocean. San Franciscans cherish the city's colorful past; many older buildings have been spared from demolition and nostalgically converted into modern offices and shops. Longtime locals rue the sites that got away—railroad and mining boom-era residences lost in the 1906 earthquake, the baroque Fox Theater, and Playland at the Beach. Despite acts of nature, the indifference of developers, and the mixed record of the city's planning commission, much of the architectural and historical interest remains. Bernard Maybeck, Julia Morgan, Willis Polk, and Arthur Brown Jr. are among the noteworthy architects whose designs remain.

UNION SQUARE AREA

Much of San Francisco may feel like a collection of small towns strung together, but the Union Square area bristles with big-city bravado. The city's finest department stores do business here, along with exclusive emporiums such as Tiffany & Co. and big-name franchises like Niketown, Planet Hollywood, Borders Books and Music, and the Virgin Megastore. Several dozen hotels within a three-block walk of the square cater to visitors. The downtown theater district and many fine arts galleries are nearby.

Numbers in the text correspond to numbers in the margin and on the Downtown San Francisco map.

What to See

🤚 ❷ **CABLE CAR TERMINUS.** San Francisco's cable cars were declared National Landmarks (the only ones that move) in 1964. Two of the three operating lines begin and end their runs in Union Square. The Powell–Mason line climbs up Nob Hill, then winds through North Beach to Fisherman's Wharf. The Powell–Hyde line also crosses Nob Hill but then continues up Russian Hill and down Hyde Street to Victorian Park, across from the Buena Vista Café and near Ghirardelli Square. Buy your ticket ($2 one-way) on board, at nearby hotels, or at the police/information booth near the turnaround. *Powell and Market Sts.*

🤚 ❼ **F.A.O. SCHWARZ.** The prices are not Toys "R" Us, but it's worth stopping by this three-floor playland to look at the 6-ft-tall stuffed animals and elaborate fairy-tale sculptures. Among the wares are an astounding supply of stuffed animals (the priciest is a whopping $15,000) and just about every other toy imaginable. *48 Stockton St., tel. 415/394–8700, www.faoschwarz.com. Daily 10–6.*

⓫ **450 SUTTER STREET.** Handsome Maya-inspired designs adorn the exterior and interior surfaces of this 1928 art deco skyscraper, a masterpiece of terra-cotta and other detailing. *Between Stockton and Powell Sts.*

❸ **GEARY THEATER.** The American Conservatory Theater (ACT), one of North America's leading repertory companies, uses the 1,035-seat Geary as its main venue. Built in 1910, the Geary has a serious neoclassic design lightened by colorful carved terra-cotta columns depicting a cornucopia of fruits. Damaged heavily in the 1989 earthquake, the Geary has been completely restored to highlight its historic, gilded splendor. *415 Geary St. (box office at 405 Geary St.), tel. 415/749–2228.*

❾ **HALLIDIE BUILDING.** Named for cable car inventor Andrew S. Hallidie, this 1918 structure is best viewed from across the street. Willis Polk's revolutionary glass-curtain wall—believed to be the world's first such facade—hangs a foot beyond the reinforced concrete of the frame. The reflecting glass, decorative exterior fire escapes that appear to be metal balconies, and Venetian Gothic cornice are worth noting. Ornamental bands of birds at feeders stretch across the building on several stories. *130 Sutter St., between Kearny and Montgomery Sts.*

⑩ HAMMERSMITH BUILDING. Glass walls and a colorful design distinguish this four-story beaux-arts–style structure, built in 1907. The Foundation for Architectural Heritage once described the building as a "commercial jewel box." Appropriately, it was originally designed for use as a jewelry store. *301 Sutter St., at Grant Ave.*

⑧ MAIDEN LANE. This former red-light district reported at least one murder a week during the late 19th century. After the 1906 fire destroyed the brothels, the street emerged as Maiden Lane, and it has since become a semi-chic pedestrian mall stretching two blocks, between Stockton and Kearny streets. Traffic is prohibited most days between 11 and 5, when the lane becomes a patchwork of umbrella-shaded tables. Masses of daffodils and balloons lend a carnival mood during the annual spring festival, when throngs of street musicians, arts-and-crafts vendors, and spectators emerge.

With its circular interior ramp and skylights, the handsome brick 1948 structure at **140 Maiden Lane,** the only Frank Lloyd Wright building in San Francisco, is said to have been his model for the Guggenheim Museum in New York. *Between Stockton and Kearny Sts.*

⑫ RUTH ASAWA'S FANTASY FOUNTAIN. Local artist Ruth Asawa's sculpture, a wonderland of real and mythical creatures, honors the city's hills, bridges, and architecture. Children and friends helped Asawa shape the hundreds of tiny figures from baker's clay; these were assembled on 41 large panels from which molds were made for the bronze casting. *In front of Grand Hyatt at 345 Stockton St.*

downtown san francisco

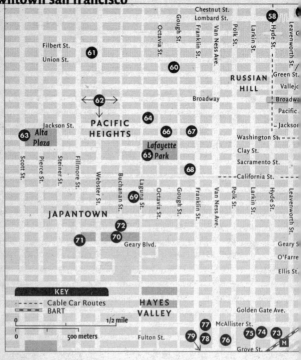

Chestnut St.
Lombard St.
reenwich St.
Filbert St.
Union St.
Columbus Ave.
Grant Ave.

San Francisco Bay

N

TELEGRAPH HILL

45 47 48
46
44
43

36
57
55

NORTH BEACH

Embarcadero

Front St.

Davis St.

St.
Tunnel
ve.
St.
Taylor St.

Powell St.
Mason St.
Stockton St.
Kearny St.
Montgomery St.
Sansome St.
Battery St.

42
41
31
30
22

54

NOB HILL

CHINATOWN

38
39 37 36 34
40
33
35 29
Halleck
28

FINANCIAL DISTRICT

Justin Herman Plaza
24

50 51 52 53
49
Pine St.

32
27

23
M
EMBARCADERO

25 26
Spear St.
Stewart St.

Bush St.
Sutter St.
Post St.

UNION SQUARE

9
11 10
M
Market St.

Beale St.
Fremont St.
Main St.

4
12
8
5
Maiden
Ln.

1st St.
2nd St.

3
7
6

21
New Montgomery St.

St.

2
19
13
3rd St.
Hawthorne St.

Eddy St.
Turk St.

SOMA
18
15 17
14

M
1

80

YERBA BUENA
16
20
Folsom St.

Market St.
Mission St.
Howard St.
6th St.
7th St.
5th St.

❶ SAN FRANCISCO VISITORS INFORMATION CENTER. A multilingual staff operates this facility below the cable car terminus. Staff members answer questions and provide maps and pamphlets. You can also pick up discount coupons—the savings can be significant, especially for families—and hotel brochures here. *Hallidie Plaza, lower level, Powell and Market Sts., tel. 415/391–2000, www.sfvisitor.org. Weekdays 9–5, weekends 9–3.*

❻ TIX BAY AREA. This excellent service provides half-price day-of-performance tickets (cash or traveler's checks only) to all types of performing arts events, as well as regular full-price box office services for theater, concerts, clubs, and sporting events (credit cards accepted). Telephone reservations are not accepted for half-price tickets. Half-price tickets for Sunday and Monday events are sold on Saturday. Also sold at the booth are Muni Passports and adult Fast Passes for use on the transit system. *Stockton St. between Geary and Post Sts., Union Square, tel. 415/433–7827, www.theatrebayarea.org. Tues.–Thurs. 11–6, Fri.–Sat. 11–7.*

❺ UNION SQUARE. The heart of San Francisco's downtown since 1850, the 2½-acre square takes its name from the violent pro-union demonstrations staged here prior to the Civil War. At center stage, the *Victory Monument*, by Robert Ingersoll Aitken, commemorates Commodore George Dewey's victory over the Spanish fleet at Manila in 1898. The 97-ft Corinthian column, topped by a bronze figure symbolizing naval conquest, was dedicated by Theodore Roosevelt in 1903 and withstood the 1906 earthquake. Once the jewel of downtown, the square looks rather dowdy nowadays. It fills daily with a familiar kaleidoscope of characters: office workers sunning and brown-bagging, street musicians, the occasional preacher, and a fair share of homeless people. *Between Powell, Stockton, Post, and Geary Sts.*

❹ WESTIN ST. FRANCIS HOTEL. The second-oldest hotel in the city, established in 1904; was conceived by railroad baron and financier Charles Crocker and his associates as a hostelry for their millionaire friends. Swift service and sumptuous surroundings—glass chandeliers, a gilt ceiling, and marble columns—have always been hallmarks of the property. After the hotel was ravaged by the 1906 fire, a larger, more luxurious Italian Renaissance-style residence was opened in 1907 to attract loyal clients from among the world's rich and powerful. The hotel's checkered past includes the ill-fated 1921 bash in the suite of the silent-film comedian Fatty Arbuckle, where a woman became ill and later died. In 1975 Sara Jane Moore, standing among a crowd outside the hotel, attempted to shoot then-president Gerald R. Ford. The ever-helpful staff will, however, direct you to tea (daily from 3 to 5) or champagne and caviar in the **Compass Rose** (tel. 415/774–0167) lounge. Elaborate Chinese screens, secluded seating alcoves, and soothing background music make this an ideal rest stop after frantic shopping or sightseeing. Reservations are not required, but walk-ins should expect a wait during December and on weekends. *335 Powell St., at Geary St., tel. 415/397–7000, www.westin.com.*

SOUTH OF MARKET (SOMA) AND THE EMBARCADERO

South of Market was once known as South of the Slot, in reference to the cable car slot that ran up Market Street. Ever since gold-rush miners set up their tents in 1848, SoMa has played a major role in housing immigrants to the city; except for a brief flowering of elegance during the mid-19th century, these streets were reserved for newcomers who couldn't yet afford to move to another neighborhood. Industry took over most of the area when the 1906 earthquake collapsed most of the homes into their quicksand bases.

Today the mood is upscale industrial. The gentrifying South Park area, recently the buzzing epicenter of new-media activity, has lost a bit of its new-economy luster in the wake of the dot-com meltdown. A mellowed cybercrowd, still outfitted with handhelds, comes here to tank up on lattes and toasted baguettes. Despite the recent influx of money, the neighborhood maintains an edge that keeps it interesting.

Numbers in the text correspond to numbers in the margin and on the Downtown San Francisco map.

What to See

㉚ ANSEL ADAMS CENTER FOR PHOTOGRAPHY. Ansel Adams created this center in Carmel in 1967, and some of his work is always on display. Exhibits have included works by contemporary Native American photographers and images of a World War II–era Japanese internment camp shot by Adams, Dorothea Lange, and Toyo Miyataki. *655 Mission St., tel. 415/495–7000, www.friendsofphotography.org. $5. Daily 11–5, 1st Thurs. of month 11–8.*

㉙ CALIFORNIA HISTORICAL SOCIETY. The society, founded in 1871, administers a vast repository of Californiana—500,000 photographs, 150,000 manuscripts, and thousands of books, periodicals, and paintings. *678 Mission St., tel. 415/357–1848, www.calhist.org. $3, free 1st Tues. of month. Tues.–Sat. 11–5 (galleries close between exhibitions).*

㉘ CARTOON ART MUSEUM. Krazy Kat, Zippy the Pinhead, Batman, and other colorful cartoon icons greet you as you walk in the door to the Cartoon Art Museum. In addition to a 12,000-piece permanent collection, a 3,000-volume library, and a CD-ROM gallery, changing exhibits examine everything from the impact of underground comics to the output of women and African-American cartoonists. *814 Mission St., 2nd floor, tel. 415/227–8666, www.cartoonart.org. $5 (pay what you wish 1st Thurs. of month). Tues.–Fri. 11–5, Sat. 10–5, Sun. 1–5.*

⑭ CENTER FOR THE ARTS. The dance, music, theater, visual arts, films, and videos presented at this facility in Yerba Buena Gardens range from the community-based to the international. *701 Mission St., tel. 415/978–2787, www.yerbabuenaarts.org. Galleries $6, free 1st*

Thurs. of month 5 PM–8 PM. Galleries and box office Tues.–Wed. and weekends 11–6, Thurs.–Fri. 11–8.

㉒ EMBARCADERO CENTER. John Portman designed this five-block complex built during the 1970s and early 1980s. Shops and restaurants abound on the first three levels; there's ample office space on the floors above. Louise Nevelson's 54-ft-high black-steel sculpture, *Sky Tree*, stands guard over Building 3 and is among 20-plus artworks throughout the center. *Clay St. between Battery St. (Embarcadero 1) and the Embarcadero (Embarcadero 5), tel. 415/772–0734, www.embarcaderocenter.com.*

㉔ FERRY BUILDING. The beacon of the port area, erected in 1896, has a 230-ft clock tower modeled after the campanile of the cathedral in Seville, Spain. On April 18, 1906, the four great clock faces on the tower, powered by the swinging of a 14-ft pendulum, stopped at 5:17—the moment the great earthquake struck—and stayed still for 12 months. While the Ferry Building is presently undergoing a $70 million renovation, a waterfront promenade that extends from the piers on the north side of the building south to the Bay Bridge is great for jogging, in-line skating, watching sailboats on the bay, or enjoying a picnic. Ferries behind the building sail to Sausalito, Larkspur, Tiburon, and the East Bay. *The Embarcadero at the foot of Market St.*

㉓ HYATT REGENCY HOTEL. John Portman designed this hotel noted for its 17-story hanging garden. Christmas is the best time to see it, when strands of tiny white lights hang down above the lobby starting at the 12th floor. The four glass elevators facing the lobby are fun to ride, unless you suffer from vertigo. The Hyatt played a starring role in the 1970s disaster movie *The Towering Inferno. Embarcadero 5, tel. 415/788–1234.*

㉖ JEWISH MUSEUM SAN FRANCISCO. The exhibits at this small museum survey Jewish art, history, and culture. Call ahead before visiting; the museum sometimes closes between exhibits. 121

Steuart St., tel. 415/788–9990, www.jmsf.org. $5, free 1st Mon. of month. Sun.–Thurs. noon–5.

⑮ METREON. Child-play meets the 21st century at this Sony entertainment center with interactive play areas based on books such as Maurice Sendak's *Where the Wild Things Are* and a three-screen, three-dimensional installation that illustrates principles discussed in architect David Macauley's *The Way Things Work*. There's also a 15-screen multiplex, an IMAX theater, retail shops, and restaurants. *4th St. between Mission and Howard Sts., tel. 800/ 638–7366, www.metreon.com.*

⑯ MOSCONE CONVENTION CENTER. The site of the 1984 Democratic convention, Moscone is distinguished by a contemporary glass-and-girder lobby at street level (all convention exhibit space is underground) and a column-free interior. *Howard St. between 3rd and 4th Sts., www.moscone.com.*

㉑ PALACE HOTEL. The city's oldest hotel opened in 1875. Fire destroyed the original Palace following the 1906 earthquake despite the hotel's 28,000-gallon reservoir fed by four artesian wells; the current building dates from 1909. President Warren Harding died at the Palace while still in office in 1923, and the body of King Kalakaua of Hawaii spent a night chilling here after he died in San Francisco in 1891. The managers play up this ghoulish past with talk of a haunted guest room. San Francisco City Guides offers free **guided tours** (tel. 415/557–4266) of the hotel's grand interior. You'll see the glass-dome Garden Court restaurant, mosaic-tile floors in Oriental rug designs, and Maxfield Parrish's wall-size painting *The Pied Piper*, the centerpiece of the Pied Piper Bar. Glass cases off the main lobby contain memorabilia of the hotel's glory days. *2 New Montgomery St., tel. 415/512–1111, www.sfpalace.com. Tours Tues. and Sat. at 10 AM, Thurs. at 2 PM.*

㉕ RINCON CENTER. A sheer five-story column of water resembling a minirainstorm stands out as the centerpiece of the indoor arcade at this mostly modern office-retail complex. The lobby of the streamline moderne–style former post office on the Mission Street side contains a Works Project Administration **mural by Anton Refregier.** The 27 panels depict California life from the days when Native Americans were the state's sole inhabitants through World War I. A permanent exhibit below the murals contains photographs and artifacts of life in the Rincon area during the 1800s. *Between Steuart, Spear, Mission, and Howard Sts.*

★ ✋ ⑰ **ROOFTOP YERBA BUENA GARDENS.** Fun is the order of the day among these brightly colored concrete and corrugated-metal buildings atop Moscone Convention Center South. A historic **Looff carousel** ($2 for two rides) twirls from Sunday to Thursday between 10 and 6, Friday and Saturday between 10 and 8. South of the carousel is **Zeum** (tel. 415/777–2800, www.zeum.org), a high-tech interactive arts and technology center ($7) geared to children ages eight and over. Zeum is open in summer Wednesday to Sunday between 11 and 5, in winter on weekends and school holidays from 11 to 5. Also part of the rooftop complex are gardens, an ice-skating rink, and a bowling alley. *4th St. between Howard and Folsom Sts.*

★ ⑬ **SAN FRANCISCO MUSEUM OF MODERN ART (SFMOMA).** Mario Botta designed the striking SFMOMA facility, completed in early 1995, which consists of a sienna brick facade and a central tower of alternating bands of black and white stone. Inside, natural light from the tower floods the central atrium and some of the museum's galleries. A black-and-gray stone staircase leads from the atrium to four floors of galleries. Works by Matisse, Picasso, O'Keeffe, Kahlo, Pollock, and Warhol form the heart of the diverse permanent collection. The adventurous programming includes traveling exhibits and multimedia installations. The café, accessible from the street, provides a comfortable, reasonably priced refuge for drinks and light meals. *151 3rd St., tel. 415/357–4000, www.sfmoma.org. $9, free 1st Tues. of each month, ½-price Thurs. 6–9. Memorial Day–Labor Day, Fri.–Tues. 10–6, Thurs. 10–9; Labor Day–Memorial Day, Fri.–Tues. 11–6, Thurs. 11–9.*

★ **YERBA BUENA GARDENS.** The centerpiece of the SoMa redevelopment area is the two blocks that encompass the Center for the Arts, Metreon, Moscone Center, and the Rooftop Yerba Buena Gardens. A circular walkway lined with benches and sculptures surrounds the East Garden, a large patch of green amid this visually stunning complex. The waterfall memorial to Martin Luther King Jr. is the focal point of the East Garden. Powerful streams of water surge over large, jagged stone columns, mirroring the enduring force of King's words that are carved on the stone walls. *Between 3rd, 4th, Mission, and Folsom Sts., www.yerbabuena.org. Daily sunrise–10 PM.*

THE HEART OF THE BARBARY COAST

The gold rush brought streams of people to San Francisco, transforming the onetime frontier town into a cosmopolitan city almost overnight. The population of San Francisco jumped from a mere 800 in 1848 to more than 25,000 in 1850, and to nearly 150,000 in 1870. Along with the prospectors came many other fortune seekers. Saloon keepers, gamblers, and prostitutes all flocked to the so-called Barbary Coast (now Jackson Square and the Financial District). Along with the quick money came a wave of violence. In 1852 the city suffered an average of two murders each day. Diarists commented that hardly a day would pass without bloodshed in the city's estimated 500 bars and 1,000 gambling dens.

By 1917 the excesses of the Barbary Coast had fallen victim to the Red-Light Abatement Act and the ire of church leaders—the wild era was over, and the young city was forced to grow up. Since then the red-light establishments have edged upward to the Broadway strip of North Beach, and Jackson Square evolved into a sedate district of refurbished brick buildings decades ago. Only one remnant of the era remains. Below Montgomery Street between California Street and Broadway, underlying many building foundations along the former waterfront area (long since filled in), lay at least 100 ships abandoned by frantic crews and passengers caught up in gold fever.

Numbers in the text correspond to numbers in the margin and on the Downtown San Francisco map.

What to See

30 JACKSON SQUARE. Here was the heart of the Barbary Coast of the Gay '90s. Though most of the red-light district was destroyed in the 1906 fire, old redbrick buildings and narrow alleys recall the romance and rowdiness of the early days. Some of the city's earliest business buildings, survivors of the 1906 quake, still stand in Jackson Square, between Montgomery and Sansome streets.

27 PACIFIC STOCK EXCHANGE. Ralph Stackpole's monumental 1930 granite sculptural groups, *Earth's Fruitfulness* and *Man's Inventive Genius*, flank this imposing structure, which dates from 1915. The Stock Exchange Tower, around the corner at 155 Sansome Street, is a 1930 modern classic by architects Miller and Pfleuger, with an art deco gold ceiling and a black marble wall entry. *301 Pine St., www.pacificex.com.*

31 SAN FRANCISCO BREWING COMPANY. Built in 1907, this pub looks like a museum piece from the Barbary Coast days. An old upright piano sits in the corner under the original stained-glass windows. Take a seat at the mahogany bar and look down at the white-tile spittoon. In an adjacent room look for the handmade copper brewing kettle used to produce a dozen beers—with such names as Pony Express—by means of old-fashioned gravity-flow methods. *155 Columbus Ave., tel. 415/434-3344, www.sfbrewing.com.*

29 TRANSAMERICA PYRAMID. The city's most photographed high-rise is the 853-ft Transamerica Pyramid. Designed by William Pereira and Associates in 1972, the initially controversial icon has become more acceptable to most locals over time. A fragrant redwood grove along the east side of the building, replete with benches and a cheerful fountain, is a placid patch in which to unwind. *600 Montgomery St., www.tapyramid.com.*

28 WELLS FARGO BANK HISTORY MUSEUM. There were no formal banks in San Francisco during the early years of the gold rush, and miners often entrusted their gold dust to saloon keepers. In 1852 Wells Fargo opened its first bank in the city, and the company established banking offices in the mother-lode camps, using stagecoaches and Pony Express riders to service the burgeoning state. The museum displays samples of nuggets and gold dust from mines, a mural-size map of the Mother Lode, original art by western artists Charles M. Russell and Maynard Dixon, mementos of the poet bandit Black Bart, and an old telegraph machine on which you can practice sending codes. The showpiece is the red Concord stagecoach, the likes of which carried passengers from St. Joseph, Missouri, to San Francisco in three weeks during the 1850s. *420 Montgomery St., tel. 415/396–2619. Free. Weekdays 9–5.*

CHINATOWN

Prepare to have your senses assaulted in Chinatown. Pungent smells waft out of restaurants, fish markets, and produce stands. Good-luck banners of crimson and gold hang beside dragon-entwined lampposts, pagoda roofs, and street signs with Chinese calligraphy. Honking cars chime in with shoppers bargaining loudly in Cantonese or Mandarin. Add to this the sight of millions of Chinese-theme goods spilling out of the shops along Grant Avenue, and you get an idea of what Chinatown is all about.

Numbers in the text correspond to numbers in the margin and on the Downtown San Francisco map.

What to See ....

32 CHINATOWN GATE. Stone lions flank the base of this pagoda-top gate, the official entrance to Chinatown and a symbolic and literal transition from the generic downtown atmosphere to what sometimes seems like another country altogether. The lions and the glazed clay dragons atop the largest of the gate's three pagodas symbolize, among other things, wealth and prosperity. The fish whose mouths wrap tightly around the crest of this pagoda symbolize prosperity. The four Chinese characters immediately beneath the pagoda represent the philosophy of Sun Yat-sen (1866–1925), the leader who unified China in the early 20th century. The vertical characters under the left pagoda read "peace" and "trust," the ones under the right pagoda "respect" and "love." *Grant Ave. at Bush St.*

39 CHINATOWN YWCA. Julia Morgan, the architect known for the famous Hearst Castle and the first woman in California to be licensed as an architect, designed this handsome redbrick building, which originally served as a meeting place and residence for Chinese women in need of social services. The YWCA building, now owned by the Chinese Historical Society, is scheduled to open as a Chinese-American history museum in mid-2001. The museum will include information on the YWCA's history and on Morgan. *965 Clay St.*

35 CHINESE CULTURE CENTER. The San Francisco Redevelopment Commission agreed to let Holiday Inn build in Chinatown if the chain provided room for a Chinese culture center. Inside the center are the works of Chinese and Chinese-American artists as well as traveling exhibits relating to Chinese culture. Walking tours ($12; make reservations one week in advance) of historic points in Chinatown take place on most days at 10 AM. *Holiday Inn, 750 Kearny St., 3rd floor, tel. 415/986–1822, www.c-c-c.org. Free. Tues.–Sun. 10–4.*

38 GOLDEN GATE FORTUNE COOKIES CO. The workers at this small factory sit at circular motorized griddles. A dollop of batter drops onto a tiny metal plate, which rotates into an oven. A few moments later out comes a cookie that's pliable and ready for folding. It's easy to peek in for a moment here. A bagful of cookies (with mildly racy "adult" fortunes or more benign ones) costs $2 or $3. 56 Ross Alley (west of and parallel to Grant Ave. between Washington and Jackson Sts.), tel. 415/781–3956. Daily 10–7.

④⓪ KONG CHOW TEMPLE. The god to whom the members of this temple pray represents honesty and trust. Chinese immigrants established the temple in 1851; its congregation moved to this building in 1977. Take the elevator up to the fourth floor, where incense fills the air. Amid the statuary, flowers, and richly colored altars (red wards off evil spirits and signifies virility, green symbolizes longevity, and gold majesty) are a couple of plaques announcing that MRS. HARRY S. TRUMAN CAME TO THIS TEMPLE IN JUNE 1948 FOR A PREDICTION ON THE OUTCOME OF THE ELECTION . . . THIS FORTUNE CAME TRUE. 855 Stockton St., no phone. Free. Mon.–Sat. 9–4.

③⑥ OLD CHINESE TELEPHONE EXCHANGE. Most of Chinatown burned down after the 1906 earthquake, and this was the first building to set the style for the new Chinatown. The intricate three-tier pagoda was built in 1909. The exchange's operators were renowned for their prodigious memories, about which the San Francisco Chamber of Commerce boasted in 1914: "These girls respond all day with hardly a mistake to calls that are given (in English or one of five Chinese dialects) by the name of the subscriber instead of by his number—a mental feat that would be practically impossible to most high-schooled American misses." Bank of Canton, 743 Washington St.

③③ OLD ST. MARY'S CATHEDRAL. This building, whose structure includes granite quarried in China, was dedicated in 1854 and served as the city's Catholic cathedral until 1891. Across California Street in **St. Mary's Park** the late local sculptor Beniamino Bufano's 12-ft-tall stainless-steel and rose-color granite statue of Sun Yat-sen towers over the site of the Chinese leader's favorite reading spot during his years in San Francisco. Grant Ave. and California St., www.oldstmarys.org.

③④ PORTSMOUTH SQUARE. Captain John B. Montgomery raised the American flag here in 1846, claiming the area from Mexico. The square—a former potato patch—was the plaza for Yerba Buena, the Mexican settlement that was renamed San Francisco. Robert Louis Stevenson, the author of *Treasure Island*, lived on the edge of Chinatown in the late 19th century and often visited this site, chatting with the sailors who hung out here. Some of the information he gleaned about life at sea found its way into his fiction. With its pagoda-shape structures, Portsmouth Square is a favorite spot for morning tai chi. By noon dozens of men huddle around Chinese chess tables, engaged in not-always-legal competition. Undercover police occasionally rush in to break things up, but this ritual, like tai chi, is an established way of life. *Bordered by Walter Lum Pl. and Kearny, Washington, and Clay Sts.*

★ ❸⑦ **TIN HOW TEMPLE.** Day Ju, one of the first three Chinese to arrive in San Francisco, dedicated this temple to the Queen of the Heavens and the Goddess of the Seven Seas in 1852. Climb three flights of stairs—on the second floor is a mah-jongg parlor whose patrons hope the spirits above will favor them. In the temple's entryway, elderly ladies can often be seen preparing "money" to be burned as offerings to various Buddhist gods or as funds for ancestors to use in the afterlife. Red-and-gold lanterns adorn the ceiling—the larger the lamp the larger its donor's contribution to the temple—and the smell of incense is usually thick. Oranges and other offerings rest on altars to various gods. *125 Waverly Pl., no phone. Free (donations accepted). Daily 9–4.*

NORTH BEACH AND TELEGRAPH HILL

Novelist and resident Herbert Gold calls North Beach "the longest-running, most glorious American bohemian operetta outside Greenwich Village." Indeed, to anyone who's spent some time in its eccentric old bars and cafés or wandered the neighborhood, North Beach evokes everything from the Barbary Coast days to the no-less-rowdy beatnik era. Italian bakeries appear frozen in time, homages to Jack Kerouac and Allen Ginsberg pop up everywhere, and the modern equivalent of the

Barbary Coast's "houses of ill repute," strip joints, do business on Broadway.

More than 125,000 Italian-American residents once lived in North Beach, but now only about 2,000, most of them elderly, do. Today the neighborhood is largely Chinese, and as local real-estate prices have escalated, a number of young professionals have moved in as well. But walk down narrow Romolo Place (off Broadway east of Columbus Avenue) or Genoa Place (off Union Street west of Kearny Street) or Medau Place (off Filbert Street west of Grant Avenue) and you can feel the immigrant Italian roots of this neighborhood.

Numbers in the text correspond to numbers in the margin and on the Downtown San Francisco map.

What to See

★ ❹ **CITY LIGHTS BOOKSTORE.** The hangout of Beat-era writers—Allen Ginsberg and Lawrence Ferlinghetti among them—remains a vital part of San Francisco's literary scene. Still leftist at heart, in 1999 the store unveiled a replica of a revolutionary mural destroyed in Chiapas, Mexico, by military forces. *261 Columbus Ave., tel. 415/362-8193, www.citylights.com.*

★ ❹ **COIT TOWER.** Among San Francisco's most distinctive skyline sights, the 210-ft-tall Coit Tower stands as a monument to the city's volunteer firefighters. During the gold rush, Lillie Hitchcock Coit (known as Miss Lil) was said to have deserted a wedding party and chased down the street after her favorite engine, Knickerbocker No. 5, while clad in her bridesmaid finery. She was soon made an honorary member of the Knickerbocker Company and after that always signed her name as "Lillie Coit 5" in honor of her favorite fire engine. Lillie died in 1929 at the age of 86, leaving the city $125,000 to "expend in an appropriate manner . . . to the beauty of San Francisco." *Telegraph Hill Blvd., at Greenwich St. or Lombard St., tel. 415/362-0808. $3.75. Daily 10-6.*

47 **JULIUS' CASTLE.** Every bit as romantic as its name implies, this contemporary Italian restaurant commands a regal view of the bay from its perch high up Telegraph Hill. An official historic landmark whose founder, Julius Roz, had his craftsmen use materials left over from the 1915 Panama–Pacific International Exposition, the restaurant has a dark-paneled Victorian interior that befits the elegant setting. *1541 Montgomery St., tel. 415/392–2222, www.juliuscastlerestaurant.com. Daily 5 PM–10 PM.*

48 **LEVI STRAUSS HEADQUARTERS.** This carefully landscaped complex appears so collegiate it is affectionately known as Levi Strauss University. *Levi's Plaza, 1155 Battery St.*

42 **ST. FRANCIS OF ASSISI CHURCH.** This 1860 building stands on the site of the frame parish church that served the Catholic community during the gold rush. Its solid terra-cotta facade complements the many brightly colored restaurants and cafés nearby. *610 Vallejo St., tel. 415/983–0405, www.shrinesf.org. Daily 11–5.*

44 **SAINTS PETER AND PAUL CATHOLIC CHURCH.** Camera-toting tourists focus their lenses on the Romanesque splendor of what's often called the Italian Cathedral. Completed in 1924, the cathedral has Disney-esque stone-white towers that are local landmarks. On the first Sunday of October a mass followed by a parade to Fisherman's Wharf celebrates the Blessing of the Fleet. *666 Filbert St., at Washington Square, www.saintspeterandpaul.com.*

45 **TELEGRAPH HILL.** Telegraph Hill got its name from one of its earliest functions—in 1853 it became the location of the first Morse Code Signal Station. Hill residents command some of the best views in the city, as well as the most difficult ascents to their aeries (the flower-lined steps flanking the hill make the climb more than tolerable for visitors, though). The Hill rises from the east end of Lombard Street to a height of 284 ft and is capped by Coit Tower. *Between Lombard, Filbert, Kearny, and Sansome Sts.*

43 WASHINGTON SQUARE. Once the daytime social heart of Little Italy, this grassy patch has changed character numerous times over the years. The Beats hung out in the 1950s, hippies camped out in the 1960s and early 1970s, and nowadays you're just as likely to see children of Southeast Asian descent tossing a Frisbee as Italian men or women chatting about their children and the old country. In the morning elderly Asians perform the motions of tai chi, but by mid-morning groups of conservatively dressed Italian men in their 70s and 80s begin to arrive. *Bordered by Columbus Ave. and Stockton, Filbert, and Union Sts.*

NOB HILL AND RUSSIAN HILL

Once called the Hill of Golden Promise, this area was officially dubbed Nob Hill during the 1870s when "the Big Four"—Charles Crocker, Leland Stanford, Mark Hopkins, and Collis Huntington, who were involved in the construction of the transcontinental railroad—built their hilltop estates. The lingo is thick from this era: those on the hilltop were referred to as "nabobs" (originally meaning a provincial governor from India) and "swells," and the hill itself was called Snob Hill, a term that survives to this day. By 1882 so many estates had sprung up on Nob Hill that Robert Louis Stevenson called it "the hill of palaces." But the 1906 earthquake and fire destroyed all the palatial mansions.

Just nine blocks or so from downtown and a few blocks north of Nob Hill, Russian Hill has long been home to old San Francisco families, who were joined during the 1890s by bohemian artists and writers that included Charles Norris, George Sterling, and Maynard Dixon. Several stories explain the origin of Russian Hill's name, though none is known to be true. One legend has it that during San Francisco's early days, the steep hill (294 ft) was the site of a cemetery for unknown Russians; another version attributes the name to a Russian sailor of prodigious drinking habits who drowned when he fell into a well on the hill. The bay views here are some of the city's best.

Numbers in the text correspond to numbers in the margin and on the Downtown San Francisco map.

What to See

★ **54** **CABLE CAR MUSEUM.** San Francisco once had more than a dozen cable car barns and powerhouses. The only survivor, this 1907 redbrick structure, an engaging stopover between Russian Hill and Nob Hill, contains photographs, old cable cars, signposts, ticketing machines, and other memorabilia dating from 1873. The massive powerhouse wheels that move the entire cable car system steal the show. The design is so simple it seems almost unreal. You can also go downstairs to the sheave room and check out the innards of the system. 1201 Mason St., at Washington St., tel. 415/474–1887, www.cablecarmuseum.com. Free. Oct.–Mar., daily 10–5; Apr.–Sept., daily 10–6.

52 **THE FAIRMONT HOTEL.** The dazzling opening was delayed a year by the 1906 quake, but since then the marble palace has hosted presidents, royalty, movie stars, and local nabobs. Prices go as high as $8,000, which buys a night in the eight-room, Persian art–filled penthouse suite that was showcased regularly in the TV series Hotel. Swing through the opulent lobby on your way to tea (served daily from 3 to 6) at the Laurel Court restaurant. Don't miss an evening cocktail (the ambience demands you order a mai tai) in the kitschy **Tonga Room,** complete with tiki huts, a sporadic tropical rainstorm, and a floating (literally) bandstand. 950 Mason St., tel. 415/772–5000, www.fairmont.com.

56 **FEUSIER HOUSE.** Octagonal houses were once thought to make the best use of space and enhance the physical and mental well-being of their occupants. A brief mid-19th-century craze inspired the construction of several in San Francisco. Only the Feusier House, built in 1857 and now a private residence surrounded by lush gardens, and the Octagon House remain standing.

50 **GRACE CATHEDRAL.** The seat of the Episcopal Church in San Francisco, this soaring Gothic structure, erected on the site of

Charles Crocker's mansion, took 53 years to build. The gilded bronze doors at the east entrance were taken from casts of Ghiberti's Gates of Paradise, which are on the baptistery in Florence, Italy. A black-and-bronze stone sculpture of St. Francis by Beniamino Bufano greets you as you enter.

The 35-ft-wide Labyrinth, a large, purplish rug, is a replica of the 13th-century stone labyrinth on the floor of the Chartres cathedral. All are encouraged to walk the ¼-mi-long labyrinth, a ritual based on the tradition of meditative walking. The AIDS Interfaith Chapel, to the right as you enter Grace, contains a sculpture by the late artist Keith Haring and panels from the AIDS Memorial Quilt. *1100 California St., at Taylor St. tel. 415/749–6300, www.gracecathedral.org. Weekdays 7–5:45, weekends 7–5.*

⑤⑤ INA COOLBRITH PARK. This attractive park is unusual because it's vertical—that is, rather than being one open space, it's composed of a series of terraces up a very steep hill. A poet, Oakland librarian, and niece of Mormon prophet Joseph Smith, for years Ina Coolbrith (1842–1928) entertained literary greats in her Macondray Lane home near the park. In 1915 she was named poet laureate of California. *Vallejo St. between Mason and Taylor Sts.*

★ **⑤⑧ LOMBARD STREET.** The block-long "Crookedest Street in the World" makes eight switchbacks down the east face of Russian Hill between Hyde and Leavenworth streets. Join the line of cars waiting to drive down the steep hill, or walk down the steps on either side of Lombard. You'll take in super views of North Beach and Coit Tower whether you walk or drive. *Lombard St. between Hyde and Leavenworth Sts.*

⑤⑦ MACONDRAY LANE. Enter this "secret garden" under a lovely wooden trellis and walk down a quiet cobbled pedestrian street lined with Edwardian cottages and flowering plants and trees. A flight of steep wooden stairs at the end of the lane leads down to Taylor Street—on the way down you can't miss the bay views.

If you've read any of Armistead Maupin's *Tales of the City* or sequels, you may find the lane vaguely familiar. *Jones St. between Union and Green Sts.*

53 **MARK HOPKINS INTER-CONTINENTAL HOTEL.** Built on the ashes of railroad tycoon Mark Hopkins's grand estate, this 19-story hotel went up in 1926. A combination of French château and Spanish Renaissance architecture, with noteworthy terra-cotta detailing, it has hosted statesmen, royalty, and Hollywood celebrities. The 11-room penthouse was turned into a glass-walled cocktail lounge in 1939: the **Top of the Mark** is remembered fondly by thousands of World War II veterans who jammed the lounge before leaving for overseas duty. Wives and sweethearts watching the ships depart gave the room's northwest nook its name—Weepers' Corner. With its 360-degree views, the lounge is a wonderful spot for a nighttime drink. *1 Nob Hill, at California and Mason Sts., tel. 415/392–3434, hotels.san-francisco.interconti.com.*

49 **MASONIC AUDITORIUM.** Formally called the California Masonic Memorial Temple, this building was erected by Freemasons in 1957. The impressive lobby mosaic, done mainly in rich greens and yellows, depicts the Masonic fraternity's role in California history and industry. There's also an intricate model of King Solomon's Temple in the lobby. *1111 California St., tel. 415/776–4702, www.sfmasoniccenter.com. Lobby weekdays 8–5.*

51 **PACIFIC UNION CLUB.** The former home of silver baron James Flood cost a whopping $1.5 million in 1886, when even a stylish Victorian such as the Haas-Lilienthal House cost less than $20,000. All that cash did buy some structural stability. The Flood residence (to be precise, its shell) was the only Nob Hill mansion to survive the 1906 earthquake and fire. The Pacific Union Club, a bastion of the wealthy and powerful, purchased the house in 1907 and commissioned Willis Polk to redesign it. *1000 California St.*

59 **SAN FRANCISCO ART INSTITUTE.** A Moorish-tile fountain in a tree-shaded courtyard immediately draws the eye as you enter the institute. The highlight of a visit is Mexican master Diego Rivera's *The Making of a Fresco Showing the Building of a City* (1931), in the student gallery to your immediate left once inside the entrance. Rivera himself is in the fresco—his back is to the viewer—and he's surrounded by his assistants.

The older portions of the Art Institute were erected in 1926. Ansel Adams created the school's fine-arts photography department in 1946, and school directors established the country's first fine-arts film program. Notable faculty and alumni have included painter Richard Diebenkorn and photographers Dorothea Lange, Edward Weston, and Annie Leibovitz. **Walter/McBean Gallery** (tel. 415/749–4563) exhibits the often provocative works of established artists. *800 Chestnut St., tel. 415/771–7020, www.sanfranciscoart.edu. Galleries free. Walter/McBean Gallery Mon.–Sat. 11–6, student gallery daily 9–9.*

PACIFIC HEIGHTS

Some of the city's most expensive and dramatic real estate—including mansions and town houses priced in the millions—is in Pacific Heights. Grand Victorians line the streets, and from almost any point in this neighborhood you get a magnificent view.

Numbers in the text correspond to numbers in the margin and on the Downtown San Francisco map.

What to See

63 **ALTA PLAZA PARK.** Landscape architect John McLaren, who also created Golden Gate Park, designed Alta Plaza in 1910, modeling its terracing on the Grand Casino in Monte Carlo, Monaco. From the top you can see Marin to the north, downtown to the east, Twin Peaks to the south, and Golden Gate Park to the west. *Between Clay, Steiner, Jackson, and Scott Sts.*

62 **BROADWAY AND WEBSTER STREET ESTATES.** Broadway uptown, unlike its garish North Beach stretch, is home to some prestigious addresses. At **2222 Broadway** is a three-story palace with an intricately filigreed doorway built by Comstock silver mine heir James Flood and later donated to a religious order. The Convent of the Sacred Heart purchased the Grant House at **2220 Broadway**. These two buildings, along with a Flood property at **2120 Broadway,** are used as school quarters. A gold mine heir, William Bourn II, commissioned Willis Polk to build the nearby mansion at **2550 Webster St.**

68 **FRANKLIN STREET BUILDINGS.** Don't be fooled by the **Golden Gate Church** (1901 Franklin St.)—what at first looks like a stone facade is actually redwood painted white. A Georgian-style residence built in the early 1900s for a coffee merchant sits at **1735 Franklin.** On the northeast corner of Franklin and California streets is a **Christian Science church**; built in the Tuscan Revival style, it's noteworthy for its terra-cotta detailing. The **Coleman House** (1701 Franklin St.) is an impressive twin-turret Queen Anne mansion built for a gold rush mining and lumber baron. Don't miss the large stained-glass window on the house's north side. *Franklin St. between Washington and California Sts.*

67 **HAAS-LILIENTHAL HOUSE.** A small display of photographs on the bottom floor of this elaborate 1886 Queen Anne house, which cost a mere $18,500 to build, makes clear that it was modest compared with some of the giants that fell victim to the 1906 earthquake and fire. The Foundation for San Francisco's Architectural Heritage operates the home, whose carefully kept rooms provide an intriguing glimpse into late 19th-century life. Volunteers conduct one-hour house tours two days a week and an informative two-hour tour of the eastern portion of Pacific Heights on Sunday afternoon. *2007 Franklin St., between Washington and Jackson Sts., tel. 415/441–3004, www.sfheritage.org/house.html. $5. Wed. noon–4 (last tour at 3), Sun. 11–5 (last tour at 4). Pacific Heights tours ($5) leave the house Sun. at 12:30.*

65 **LAFAYETTE PARK.** Clusters of trees dot this four-block-square oasis for sunbathers and dog-and-Frisbee teams. *Between Laguna, Gough, Sacramento, and Washington Sts.*

69 NOTEWORTHY VICTORIANS. Two **Italianate Victorians** (1818 and 1834 California St.) stand out on the 1800 block of California. A block farther is the Victorian-era **Atherton House** (1990 California St.), whose mildly daffy design incorporates Queen Anne, Stick-Eastlake, and other architectural elements. The oft-photographed **Laguna Street Victorians,** on the west side of the 1800 block of Laguna Street, cost between $2,000 and $2,600 when they were built in the 1870s. *California St. between Franklin and Octavia Sts., and Laguna St. between Pine and Bush Sts.*

60 OCTAGON HOUSE. This eight-sided home sits across the street from its original site on Gough Street. It's full of antique American furniture, decorative arts (paintings, silver, rugs), and documents from the 18th and 19th centuries. White quoins accent each of the eight corners of the pretty blue-gray exterior. An award-winning Colonial-style garden completes the picture. *2645 Gough St., tel. 415/441–7512. Free (donations encouraged). Feb.–Dec., 2nd Sun. and 2nd and 4th Thurs. of each month noon–3; group tours weekdays by appointment.*

66 SPRECKELS MANSION. This estate was built for sugar heir Adolph Spreckels and his wife, Alma. Mrs. Spreckels was so pleased with her house that she commissioned George Applegarth to design another building in a similar vein: the California Palace of the Legion of Honor. *2080 Washington St., at Octavia St.*

61 VEDANTA SOCIETY. A pastiche of Colonial, Queen Anne, Moorish, and Hindu opulence, with turrets battling onion domes and Victorian detailing everywhere, this 1905 structure was the first Hindu temple in the West. *2963 Webster St., tel. 415/922–2323, www.sfvedanta.com.*

WEDDING HOUSES. These identical white double-peak homes (joined in the middle) were erected in the late 1870s or early 1880s by dairy rancher James Cudworth as wedding gifts for his two daughters. *1980 Union St.*

64 **WHITTIER MANSION.** This was one of the most elegant 19th-century houses in the state, with a Spanish-tile roof and scrolled bay windows on all four sides. An anomaly in a town that lost most of its grand mansions to the 1906 quake, the Whittier Mansion was built so solidly that only a chimney toppled over during the disaster. *2090 Jackson St.*

JAPANTOWN

Around 1860 a wave of Japanese immigrants arrived in San Francisco, which they called Soko. After the 1906 earthquake and fire, many of these newcomers settled in the Western Addition. By the 1930s they had opened shops, markets, meeting halls, and restaurants and established Shinto and Buddhist temples. Known as Japantown, this area was virtually deserted during World War II when many of its residents, including second- and third-generation Americans, were forced into so-called relocation camps. Today Japantown, or Nihonmachi, is centered on the southern slope of Pacific Heights, north of Geary Boulevard between Fillmore and Laguna streets. The Nihonmachi Cherry Blossom Festival is celebrated on two weekends in April.

Numbers in the text correspond to numbers in the margin and on the Downtown San Francisco map.

What to See

70 **JAPAN CENTER.** The noted American architect Minoru Yamasaki created this 5-acre complex, which opened in 1968. The development includes a hotel (the Radisson Miyako, at Laguna and Post streets); shops selling Japanese furnishings, clothing, cameras, tapes and records, porcelain, pearls, and paintings; an excellent spa; and a multiplex cinema.

72 **JAPAN CENTER MALL.** The buildings lining this open-air mall are of the shoji school of architecture. Seating in this area can be found on local artist Ruth Asawa's twin origami-style fountains, which sit in the middle of the mall; they're squat circular structures made of fieldstone. *Buchanan St. between Post and Sutter Sts.*

★ ⓐ **KABUKI SPRINGS & SPA.** Japantown's house of tranquility got a complete makeover in 1999. The feel is less Japanese than before. Balinese urns decorate the communal bath area, and you're just as likely to hear soothing flute or classical music as you are Kitaro. The massage palette has also expanded well beyond the traditional shiatsu technique. The experience is no less relaxing, however, and the treatment regimen now includes facials, salt scrubs, and mud and seaweed wraps. You can take your massage in a private room with a bath or in a curtained-off area. The communal baths ($12 before 5 PM, $16 after 5 and all weekend) contain hot and cold tubs, a large Japanese-style bath, a sauna, a steam room, and showers. The baths are open for men only on Monday, Thursday, and Saturday, and for women only on Wednesday, Friday, and Sunday. A 90-minute massage-and-bath package with a private room costs $90. A package that includes a 50-minute massage and the use of the communal baths costs $75. *1750 Geary Blvd., tel. 415/922–6000, www.kabukisprings.com. Daily 10–10.*

CIVIC CENTER

The Civic Center—the beaux-arts complex between McAllister and Grove streets and Franklin and Hyde streets that includes City Hall, the War Memorial Opera House, the Veterans Building, and the old Public Library (slated to become the Asian Art Museum and Cultural Center in the fall of 2002)—is a product of the "City Beautiful" movement of the early 20th century. City Hall, completed in 1915 and renovated in 1999, is the centerpiece.

Numbers in the text correspond to numbers in the margin and on the Downtown San Francisco map.

What to See

★ ⓻ **ASIAN ART MUSEUM.** In the fall of 2002 the Asian Art Museum, one of the largest collections of Asian art in the world, opens in its new home (it is no longer open in its previous Golden Gate Park location). Holdings include more than 12,000 sculptures, paintings, and ceramics from 40 countries, illustrating major periods of Asian art. Though the bulk of the art and artifacts come from China, treasures from Korea, Iran, Turkey, Syria, India, Tibet, Nepal, Pakistan, India, Japan, Afghanistan, and Southeast Asia are also on view. *200 Larkin St., between McAllister and Fulton Sts. (as of fall 2002), tel. 415/668–8921 or 415/379–8801, www.asianart.org. $7, free 1st Wed. of month. Wed.–Sun. 9:30–5, 1st Wed. of month until 8:45.*

76 **CITY HALL.** This masterpiece of granite and marble was modeled after St. Peter's Cathedral in Rome. City Hall's bronze and gold-leaf dome, which is even higher than the U.S. Capitol's version, dominates the area. Some noteworthy events that have taken place here include the marriage of Marilyn Monroe and Joe DiMaggio (1954); the hosing—down the central staircase—of civil rights and freedom of speech protesters (1960); the murders of Mayor George Moscone and openly gay supervisor Harvey Milk (1978); the torching of the lobby by angry members of the gay community in response to the light sentence given to the former supervisor who killed them (1979); and the weddings of scores of gay couples in celebration of the passage of San Francisco's Domestic Partners Act (1991). The palatial interior, full of grand arches and with a sweeping central staircase, is impressive. Free tours are also available weekdays at 10, noon, and 2 and weekends at 12:30. The **Museum of the City of San Francisco** (tel. 415/928–0289), on the third floor, displays historical items, maps, and photographs, as well as the 500-pound head of the Goddess of Progress statue, which crowned the City Hall building that crumbled during the 1906 earthquake. Admission to the museum is free. Across Polk Street is **Civic Center Plaza,** with lawns, walkways, seasonal flower beds, and a playground. *Between Van Ness Ave. and Polk, Grove, and McAllister Sts., tel. 415/554–6023, www.ci.sf.ca.us/cityhall.*

79 LOUISE M. DAVIES SYMPHONY HALL. Fascinating and futuristic looking, this 2,750-seat hall is the home of the San Francisco Symphony. The glass wraparound lobby and pop-out balcony high on the southeast corner are visible from the outside. Henry Moore created the bronze sculpture that sits on the sidewalk at Van Ness Avenue and Grove Street. The hall's 59 adjustable Plexiglas acoustical disks cascade from the ceiling like hanging windshields. Scheduled tours (75 minutes), which meet at the Grove Street entrance, take in Davies and the nearby opera house and Herbst Theatre. *201 Van Ness Ave., tel. 415/552–8338. Tours $5. Tours Mon. on the hr 10–2.*

74 SAN FRANCISCO PUBLIC LIBRARY. The main library, which opened in 1996, is a modernized version of the old beaux-arts library that sits just across Fulton Street. The several specialty rooms include centers for the hearing and visually impaired, a gay and lesbian history center, and African-American and Asian centers. At the library's core is a five-story atrium with a skylight, a grand staircase, and murals painted by local artists. Tours of the library are conducted Wednesday, Friday, and Saturday at 2:30 PM. *100 Larkin St., between Grove and Fulton Sts., tel. 415/557–4400, www.sfpl.lib.ca.us. Mon. and Sat. 10–6, Tues.–Thurs. 9–8, Fri. noon–6, Sun. noon–5.*

73 UNITED NATIONS PLAZA. This monument is inscribed with the goals and philosophy of the United Nations charter, which was signed at the War Memorial Opera House in 1945. On Wednesday and Sunday a farmers' market fills the space with homegrown produce and plants. *Fulton St. between Hyde and Market Sts.*

77 VETERANS BUILDING. Performing and visual arts organizations occupy much of this 1930s structure. **Herbst Theatre** (tel. 415/392–4400) hosts lectures, music, and dance performances. The street-level **San Francisco Arts Commission Gallery** (tel. 415/554–6080), open from Wednesday to Saturday between noon and 5:30, displays the works of Bay Area artists. The **San Francisco**

Performing Arts Library and Museum (tel. 415/255–4800) on the fourth floor functions mainly as a research center, documenting and preserving the San Francisco Bay Area's rich performing arts legacy. The gallery is open Tuesday and Thursday 11–5, Wednesday 11–7. *401 Van Ness Ave.*

㊲ **WAR MEMORIAL OPERA HOUSE.** During San Francisco's Barbary Coast days, operagoers smoked cigars, didn't check their revolvers, and expressed their appreciation with "shrill whistles and savage yells," as one observer put it. All the old opera houses were destroyed in the 1906 quake, but lusty support for opera continued. Modeled after its European counterparts, the building has a vaulted and coffered ceiling, marble foyer, two balconies, and a huge silver art deco chandelier that resembles a sunburst. *301 Van Ness Ave., tel. 415/621–6600.*

THE NORTHERN WATERFRONT

For the sights, sounds, and smells of the sea, hop the Powell–Hyde cable car from Union Square and take it to the end of the line. The views as you descend Hyde Street down to the bay are breathtaking—tiny sailboats bob in the whitecaps, Alcatraz hovers ominously in the distance, and the Marin Headlands form a rugged backdrop to the Golden Gate Bridge. Once you reach sea level at the cable car turnaround, Aquatic Park and the National Maritime Museum are immediately to the west, and the commercial attractions of the Fisherman's Wharf area are to the east. Bring good walking shoes and a jacket or sweater for mid-afternoon breezes or foggy mists.

Numbers in the text correspond to numbers in the margin and on the Northern Waterfront/Marina and the Presidio map.

What to See

★ **ALCATRAZ ISLAND.** The boat ride to the island is brief (15 minutes) but affords beautiful views of the city, Marin County, and the East Bay. The audio tour, highly recommended,

northern waterfront/marina and the presidio

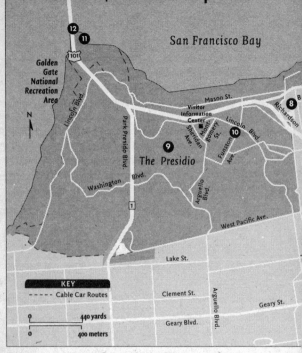

Cannery, 4	Golden Gate Bridge, 12	Pier 39, 6
Fisherman's Wharf, 5	Hyde Street Pier, 3	Presidio, 9
Fort Mason Center, 7	National Maritime Museum, 1	Presidio Visitor Center, 10
Fort Point, 11	Palace of Fine Arts, 8	
Ghirardelli Square, 2		

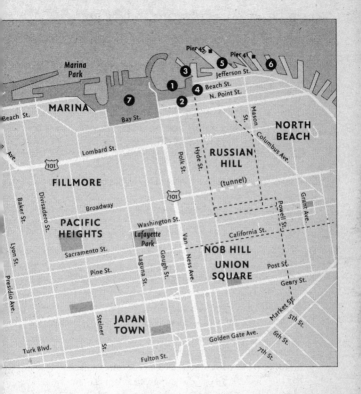

Pier 45 ■

Pier 41 ■

3

5

Jefferson St.

1

6

Marina
Park

2

4

Beach St.

N. Point St.

7

MARINA

Bay St.

Beach St.

Mason St.

**NORTH
BEACH**

Columbus Ave.

Lombard St.

Polk St.

Hyde St.

**RUSSIAN
HILL**

101

(tunnel)

FILLMORE

Broadway

101

Grant Ave.

Baker St.

Divisadero St.

**PACIFIC
HEIGHTS**

Washington St.

*Lafayette
Park*

California St.

Powell St.

Lyon St.

Sacramento St.

Laguna St.

Van Ness Ave.

Gough St.

NOB HILL

**UNION
SQUARE**

Post St.

Presidio Ave.

Pine St.

Geary St.

Market St.

5th St.

**JAPAN
TOWN**

Steiner St.

Golden Gate Ave.

6th St.

Turk Blvd.

7th St.

Fulton St.

includes observations of guards and prisoners about life in one of America's most notorious penal colonies. Plan your schedule to allow at least three hours for the visit and boat rides combined. Reservations, even in the off-season, are recommended. *Pier 41, tel. 415/773–1188 boat schedules and information; 415/705–5555 or 800/426–8687 credit-card ticket orders; 415/705–1042 park information, www.nps.gov/alcatraz. $12.25, $9 without audio ($19.75 evening tours, including audio); add $2.25 per ticket to charge by phone. Ferry departures Sept.–late May, daily 9:30–2:15 (4:20 for evening tour Thurs.–Sun. only); late May–Aug., daily 9:30–4:15 (6:30 and 7:30 for evening tour).*

❹ CANNERY. This three-story structure was built in 1894 to house what became the Del Monte Fruit and Vegetable Cannery. Today the Cannery is home to shops, art galleries, a comedy club (Cobb's), and some unusual restaurants. *2801 Leavenworth St., tel. 415/771–3112.*

❺ FISHERMAN'S WHARF. Ships creak at their moorings; seagulls cry out for a handout. By mid-afternoon the fishing fleet is back to port. The chaotic streets of the wharf are home to numerous seafood restaurants, among them sidewalk stands where shrimp and crab cocktails are sold in disposable containers. T-shirts and sweats, gold chains galore, redwood furniture, and acres of artwork (precious little of it original) also beckon visitors. Everything's overpriced, especially the so-called novelty museums, which can provide a diversion if you're touring with antsy children. The best of the lot, though mostly for its kitsch value, is **Ripley's Believe It or Not! Museum** (175 Jefferson St., tel. 415/439–4305). For an intriguing if mildly claustrophobic glimpse into life on a submarine during World War II, drop by the **USS Pampanito** (Pier 45, tel. 415/775–1943). The sub, open Monday–Thursday 9–6, Friday–Sunday 9–8, sank six Japanese warships and damaged four others. Admission is $7. *Jefferson St. between Leavenworth St. and Pier 39.*

❷ GHIRARDELLI SQUARE. Most of the redbrick buildings in this early 20th-century complex were part of the Ghirardelli chocolate factory. Now they house name-brand emporiums, restaurants, and galleries that sell everything from crafts and knickknacks to sports memorabilia. Placards throughout the square describe the factory's history. *900 N. Point St., tel. 415/775–5500.*

❸ HYDE STREET PIER. The pier, one of the wharf area's best bargains, always crackles with activity. The highlight of the pier is its collection of historic vessels, all of which can be boarded: the *Balclutha*, an 1886 full-rigged three-masted sailing vessel that sailed around Cape Horn 17 times; the *Eureka*, a side-wheel ferry; the *C. A. Thayer*, a three-masted schooner; and the *Hercules*, a steam-powered tugboat. *Hyde and Jefferson Sts., tel. 415/556–3002 or 415/556–0859. $5. Daily 9:30–5.*

❶ NATIONAL MARITIME MUSEUM. You'll feel as if you're out to sea when you step inside this sturdy, rounded structure. Part of the San Francisco Maritime National Historical Park, which includes Hyde Street Pier, the museum exhibits ship models, maps, and other artifacts chronicling the development of San Francisco and the West Coast through maritime history. *Aquatic Park at the foot of Polk St., tel. 415/556–3002, www.nps.gov. Donation suggested. Daily 10–5.*

❻ PIER 39. This is the most popular—and commercial—of San Francisco's waterfront attractions, drawing millions of visitors each year to browse through its dozens of shops. Check out the **Marine Mammal Store & Interpretive Center** (tel. 415/289–7373), a quality gift shop and education center whose proceeds benefit Sausalito's Marine Mammal Center, and the **National Park Store** (tel. 415/433–7221), with books, maps, and collectibles sold to support the National Park Service. Brilliant colors enliven the double-decker **Venetian Carousel,** often awhirl with happily howling children ($2 a ride). The din on the northwest side of the pier comes courtesy of the hundreds of sea lions that bask and play on the docks. At **Underwater World** (tel. 415/623–5300 or 888/732–3483), moving walkways transport you through a space surrounded on three sides by water filled with indigenous San

Francisco Bay marine life, from fish and plankton to sharks. *Beach St. at the Embarcadero., www.pier39.com.*

THE MARINA AND THE PRESIDIO

The Marina district was a coveted place to live until the 1989 earthquake, when the area's homes suffered the worst damage in the city—largely because the Marina is built on landfill. Many homeowners and renters fled in search of more solid ground, but young professionals quickly replaced them, changing the tenor of this formerly low-key neighborhood. The number of upscale coffee emporiums skyrocketed. A bank became a Williams-Sonoma and the local grocer gave way to a Pottery Barn.

West of the Marina is the sprawling Presidio, a former military base. The Presidio has superb views and the best hiking and biking areas in San Francisco; a drive through the area can also be rewarding.

Numbers in the text correspond to numbers in the margin and on the Northern Waterfront/Marina and the Presidio map.

What to See

★ ☺ **EXPLORATORIUM.** The curious of all ages flock to this fascinating "museum of science, art, and human perception" within the Palace of Fine Arts. The more than 650 exhibits focus on sea and insect life, computers, electricity, patterns and light, language, the weather, and much more. Reservations are required to crawl through the pitch-black, touchy-feely **Tactile Dome,** an adventure of 15 minutes. The object is to crawl and climb through the space relying solely on the sense of touch. *3601 Lyon St., at Marina Blvd., tel. 415/561–0360 general information; 415/561–0362 Tactile Dome reservations, www.exploratorium.edu. $9, free 1st Wed. of month; Tactile Dome $3 extra. Memorial Day–Labor Day, Sun.–Tues. and Thurs.–Sat. 10–6, Wed. 10–9; Labor Day–Memorial Day, Tues. and Thurs.–Sun. 10–5, Wed. 10–9.*

7 **FORT MASON CENTER.** Originally a depot for the shipment of supplies to the Pacific during World War II, Fort Mason was converted into a cultural center in 1977. It houses several worthwhile museums. The **Museo Italo-Americano** (tel. 415/673–2200) mounts impressive exhibits of the works of Italian and Italian-American artists. The exhibits at the **San Francisco African-American Historical and Cultural Society** (tel. 415/441–0640) document past and contemporary black arts and culture. The **San Francisco Craft and Folk Art Museum** (tel. 415/775–0990) is an airy space with exhibits of American folk art, tribal art, and contemporary crafts. Next door is the **SFMOMA Rental Gallery** (tel. 415/441–4777), where the art is available for sale or rent. Most of the museums and shops at Fort Mason close by 6 or 7. The museum admission fees range from pay-what-you-wish to $4. *Buchanan St. and Marina Blvd., tel. 415/979–3010 event information.*

11 **FORT POINT.** Designed to mount 126 cannons with a range of up to 2 mi, Fort Point was constructed between 1853 and 1861 to protect San Francisco from sea attack during the Civil War—but it was never used for that purpose. It was, however, used as a coastal defense fortification post during World War II, when soldiers stood watch here. This National Historic Site is a museum filled with military memorabilia. The building has a gloomy air and is suitably atmospheric. On days when Fort Point is staffed, guided group tours and cannon drills take place. *Marine Dr. off Lincoln Blvd., tel. 415/556–1693, www.nps.gov/fopo. Free. Thurs.–Mon. 10–5.*

★ **12** **GOLDEN GATE BRIDGE.** The suspension bridge that connects San Francisco with Marin County has long wowed sightseers with its rust-color beauty, 750-ft towers, and simple but powerful art deco design. At nearly 2 mi, the Golden Gate, completed in 1937 after four years of construction, was built to withstand winds of more than 100 mph. The east walkway yields a glimpse of the San Francisco skyline as well as the islands of the bay. The view west takes in the wild hills of the Marin Headlands, the curving coast south to Land's End, and the majestic Pacific Ocean. A vista point on the Marin side affords a spectacular view of the city. On sunny days sailboats dot the water, and brave windsurfers test the often-treacherous tides beneath the bridge. Muni Buses 28 and 29 make stops at the Golden Gate Bridge toll plaza, on the San Francisco side. *Lincoln Blvd. near Doyle Dr. and Fort Point, tel. 415/ 921–5858, www.goldengate.org. Daily; 5 AM–9 PM for pedestrians.*

★ **8 PALACE OF FINE ARTS.** San Francisco's rosy rococo Palace of Fine Arts is at the western end of the Marina. The palace is the sole survivor of the many tinted plaster buildings (a temporary classical city of sorts) built for the 1915 Panama-Pacific International Exposition, the world's fair that celebrated San Francisco's recovery from the 1906 earthquake and fire. The expo lasted for 288 days and the buildings extended about a mile along the shore. Bernard Maybeck designed this faux Roman Classic beauty, which was reconstructed in concrete and reopened in 1967. *Baker and Beach Sts., tel. 415/561–0364 palace tours, www.exploratorium. edu/palace.*

9 PRESIDIO. Part of the Golden Gate National Recreation Area, the Presidio was a military post for more than 200 years. Don Juan Bautista de Anza and a band of Spanish settlers first claimed the area in 1776. It became a Mexican garrison in 1822 when Mexico gained its independence from Spain; U.S. troops forcibly occupied the Presidio in 1846. The U.S. Sixth Army was stationed here until October 1994, when the coveted space was transferred into civilian hands. The more than 1,400 acres of rolling hills, majestic woods, and redbrick army barracks present an air of serenity on the edge of the city. There are two beaches, a golf course, a visitor center, and picnic sites, and the views of the bay, the Golden Gate Bridge, and Marin County are sublime. *Between the Marina and Lincoln Park, www.nps.gov/prsf.*

10 PRESIDIO VISITOR CENTER. National Park Service employees at what's officially the William P. Mott Jr. Visitor Center dispense maps, brochures, and schedules for guided walking and bicycle tours, along with information about the Presidio's past, present, and future. The building also houses the **Presidio Museum**, which focuses on the role played by the military in San Francisco's development. *Montgomery St. between Lincoln Blvd. and Sheridan Ave., tel. 415/561–4323. Free. Daily 9–5.*

GOLDEN GATE PARK

William Hammond Hall conceived one of the nation's great city parks and began in 1870 to put into action his plan for a natural reserve with no reminders of urban life. Hammond began work in the Panhandle and eastern portions of Golden Gate Park, but it took John McLaren the length of his tenure as park superintendent, from 1890 to 1943, to complete the transformation of 1,000 desolate brush- and sand-covered acres into a rolling, landscaped oasis. On Sunday John F. Kennedy Drive is closed to cars and comes alive with joggers, cyclists, and in-line skaters. In addition to cultural and other attractions there are public tennis courts, baseball diamonds, soccer fields, and trails for horseback riding. The fog can sweep into the park with amazing speed; always bring a sweatshirt or jacket.

Because the park is so large, a car will come in handy if you're going to tour it from one end to the other. Muni also serves the park. Buses 5-Fulton and 21-Hayes stop along its northern edge, and the N-Judah light-rail car stops a block south of the park between Stanyan Street and 9th Avenue, then two blocks south and the rest of the way west.

Numbers in the text correspond to numbers in the margin and on the Golden Gate Park map.

What to See

⓾ **BEACH CHALET.** This Spanish colonial–style structure, architect Willis Polk's last design, was built in 1925 after his death. A wraparound Federal Works Project mural by Lucien Labaudt

golden gate park

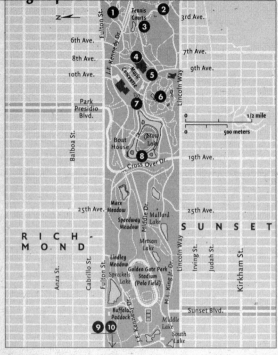

depicts San Francisco in the 1930s; the labels describing the various panels add up to a minihistory of Depression-era life in the city. A three-dimensional model of Golden Gate Park, artifacts from the 1894 Mid-Winter Exposition and other park events, a visitor center, and a gift shop that sells street signs and other city paraphernalia are on the first floor as well. On a clear day, the brewpub-restaurant upstairs has views past Ocean Beach to the Farallon Islands, about 30 mi offshore. *1000 Great Hwy., at west end of John F. Kennedy Dr., www.beachchalet.com.*

BUFFALO PADDOCK. The original denizens of the paddock arrived at the park in 1894 for the Mid-Winter Exposition. The present herd, from Wyoming, was acquired in 1984. *John F. Kennedy Dr. west of Spreckels Lake.*

★ **CALIFORNIA ACADEMY OF SCIENCES.** A three-in-one attraction, the nationally renowned academy houses an aquarium, numerous science and natural-history exhibits, and a planetarium. Leopard sharks, silver salmon, sea bass, and other fish loop around the mesmerizing Fish Roundabout, the big draw at **Steinhart Aquarium.** Feeding time is 1:30 PM. At the Touch Tide Pool, you can cozy up to starfish, hermit crabs, and other critters. Elsewhere at Steinhart swim dolphins, sea turtles, piranhas, manatees, and other sea life. The multimedia earthquake exhibit in the Earth and Space Hall at the **Natural History Museum** simulates quakes, complete with special effects. Videos and displays in the Wild California Hall describe the state's wildlife, and there's a re-creation of the environment of the rocky Farallon Islands. There is an additional charge ($2.50) for **Morrison Planetarium** shows (tel. 415/750–7141 for schedule), which you enter through the Natural History Museum. Daily multimedia shows present the night sky through the ages under a 55-ft dome, complete with special effects and music. A cafeteria is open daily until one hour before the museum closes. *Music Concourse Dr. off South Dr., tel. 415/750–7145, www.calacademy.org.* $8.50 ($2.50 discount with Muni transfer), free 1st Wed. of month.

Memorial Day–Labor Day, daily 9–6; Labor Day–Memorial Day, daily 10–5; 1st Wed. of month closes at 8:45 PM.

② CHILDREN'S PLAYGROUND. A menagerie of handcrafted horses and other animals—among them cats, frogs, roosters, and a tiger—twirl on the 1912 Herschell-Spillman Carousel, inside a many-windowed circular structure. The Romanesque-style Sharon Building looms over the playground. The 1887 structure has been rebuilt twice, following the earthquake of 1906 and a 1980 fire. *Bowling Green Dr., off Martin Luther King Jr. Dr., tel. 415/753–5210 or 415/831–2700. Playground free, carousel $1. Playground daily dawn–midnight; carousel June–Sept., daily 10–5; Oct.–May, Fri.–Sun. 9–4.*

① CONSERVATORY OF FLOWERS. The oldest building in the park and the last remaining wood-frame Victorian conservatory in the country, the Conservatory, which was built in the late 1870s, is a copy of the one in the Royal Botanical Gardens in Kew, England. On the east side of the Conservatory (to the right as you face the building), cypress, pine, and redwood trees surround the **Fuchsia Garden,** which blooms in summer and fall. To the west several hundred feet on John F. Kennedy Drive is the **Rhododendron Dell.** The dell contains the most varieties—850 in all—of any garden in the country. *John F. Kennedy Dr. at Conservatory Dr.*

⑨ DUTCH WINDMILL. The restored 1902 Dutch Windmill once pumped 20,000 gallons of well water per hour to the reservoir on Strawberry Hill. With its heavy cement bottom and wood-shingled arms and upper section the windmill cuts quite the sturdy figure. The structure overlooks the equally photogenic **Queen Wilhelmina Tulip Garden,** which bursts into full bloom in early spring and late summer. *Between 47th Ave. and the Great Hwy.*

★ ⑦ JAPANESE TEA GARDEN. A serene 4-acre landscape of small ponds, streams, waterfalls, stone bridges, Japanese sculptures, *mumsai* (planted bonsai) trees, perfect miniature pagodas, and some nearly vertical wooden "humpback" bridges, the tea garden was created for the 1894 Mid-Winter Exposition. *Tea Garden Dr. off John F. Kennedy Dr., tel. 415/752–4227 or 415/752–1171. $3.50. Mar.– Sept., daily 9–6:30; Oct.–Feb., daily 8:30–5:30.*

❸ NATIONAL AIDS MEMORIAL GROVE. This 15-acre grove, started in the early 1990s by people with AIDS and their families and friends, was conceived as a living memorial to those the disease has claimed. Hundreds of volunteers toiled long and hard raising funds and clearing this patch of green. A 1996 poem by San Franciscan Thom Gunn in the tan fieldstone circle at the west end of the grove reads: WALKER WITHIN THIS CIRCLE PAUSE/ALTHOUGH THEY DIED OF ONE CAUSE/REMEMBER HOW THEIR LIVES WERE DENSE/WITH FINE COMPACTED DIFFERENCE. *Middle Dr. E, west of tennis courts, www.aidsmemorial.org.*

❺ SHAKESPEARE GARDEN. Two hundred flowers and herbs mentioned in the Bard's plays grow here. Bronze-engraved passages contain relevant floral quotations. *Middle Dr. E at southwest corner of California Academy of Sciences.*

❽ STOW LAKE. One of the most picturesque spots in Golden Gate Park, this placid body of water surrounds Strawberry Hill. A couple of bridges allow you to cross over and ascend the hill. Down below, rent a boat, surrey, or bicycle or stroll around the perimeter. *Off John F. Kennedy Dr., ½ mi west of 10th Ave., tel. 415/752–0347.*

❻ STRYBING ARBORETUM & BOTANICAL GARDENS. The 55-acre arboretum specializes in plants from areas with climates similar to that of the Bay Area, such as the west coast of Australia, South Africa, and the Mediterranean; more than 8,000 plant and tree varieties bloom in gardens throughout the grounds. Among the highlights are the Biblical, Fragrance, California Native Plants, Succulents, and Primitive Plant gardens, the new- and old-world cloud forests, and the duck pond. *9th Ave. at Lincoln Way, tel. 415/ 661–1316, www.strybing.org. Free. Weekdays 8–4:30, weekends 10–5. Tours from bookstore weekdays at 1:30, weekends at 10:30 and 1:30.*

LINCOLN PARK AND THE WESTERN SHORELINE

From Land's End in Lincoln Park you'll have some of the best views of the Golden Gate (the name was originally given to the opening of San Francisco Bay long before the bridge was built) and the Marin Headlands. From the historic Cliff House south to the sprawling San Francisco Zoo, the Great Highway and Ocean Beach run along the western edge of the city. The wind is often strong along the shoreline, summer fog can blanket the ocean beaches, and the water is cold and usually too rough for swimming. Carry a jacket and bring binoculars.

Numbers in the text correspond to numbers in the margin and on the Lincoln Park and the Western Shoreline map.

What to See

★ ❷ **CALIFORNIA PALACE OF THE LEGION OF HONOR.** Spectacularly situated on cliffs overlooking the ocean, the Golden Gate Bridge, and the Marin Headlands, this landmark building is a fine repository of European art. A pyramidal glass skylight in the entrance court illuminates the lower-level galleries, which exhibit prints and drawings; English and European porcelain; and ancient Assyrian, Greek, Roman, and Egyptian art. The 20-plus galleries on the upper level display the permanent collection of European art from the 14th century to the present day. The noteworthy Rodin collection includes two galleries devoted to the master and a third with works by Rodin and other 19th-century sculptors. An original cast of Rodin's *The Thinker* welcomes you as you walk through the courtyard. The **Legion Café**, on the lower level, has a garden terrace and a view of the Golden Gate Bridge. North of the museum (across Camino del Mar) is George Segal's *The Holocaust*, a sculpture that evokes life in concentration camps during World War II. *34th Ave. at Clement St., tel. 415/863–3330 information, www.thinker.org. $8 ($2 off with Muni transfer), good also for same-day admission to Asian Art Museum; free 2nd Wed. of month. Tues.–Sun. 9:30–5.*

④ CLIFF HOUSE. Three buildings have occupied this site since 1863. The original Cliff House hosted several U.S. presidents and wealthy locals who would drive their carriages out to Ocean Beach; it was destroyed by fire on Christmas Day 1894. The second Cliff House, the most beloved and resplendent of the three, was built in 1896; it rose eight stories with an observation tower 200 ft above sea level. The current building dates from 1909. The complex, which includes restaurants, a pub, and a gift shop, remains open while undergoing a gradual renovation to restore its early 20th-century look. The dining areas overlook Seal Rock (the barking marine mammals sunning themselves are actually sea lions).

Below the Cliff House is the splendid **Musée Mécanique** (tel. 415/386–1170), a time-warped arcade with antique mechanical contrivances, including peep shows and nickelodeons. Some favorites are the giant, rather creepy "Laughing Sal," an arm-wrestling machine, and mechanical fortune-telling figures who speak from their curtained boxes. The museum opens daily from Memorial Day to Labor Day between 10 and 8 and the rest of the year on weekdays between 11 and 7 and on weekends between 10 and 8. Admission is free, but you may want to bring change to play the games.

The Musée Mécanique looks out on a fine observation deck and the **Golden Gate National Recreation Area Visitors' Center** (tel. 415/556–8642, www.nps.gov/goga), which contains fascinating historical photographs of the Cliff House and the glass-roof Sutro Baths. The Sutro complex, which comprised six enormous baths, 500 dressing rooms, and several restaurants, covered 3 acres north of the Cliff House. The baths burned down in 1966. You can explore the ruins on your own or take ranger-led walks on weekends. *1090 Point Lobos Ave., tel. 415/386–3330, www.cliffhouse.com and www.nps.gov/goga/clho. Weekdays 8 AM–10:30 PM, weekends 8 AM–11 PM; cocktails served nightly until 2 AM.*

① LINCOLN PARK. At one time most of the city's cemeteries were here, segregated by nationality. In 1900, the Board of Supervisors

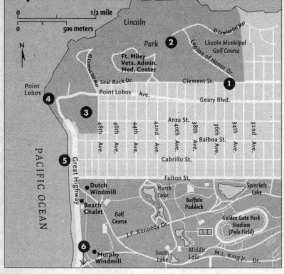

California Palace
of the Legion
of Honor, 2

Cliff House, 4

Lincoln Park, 1

Ocean
Beach, 5

San Francisco
Zoo, 6

Sutro Heights
Park, 3

voted to ban burials within city limits. Large Monterey cypresses line the fairways at Lincoln Park's 18-hole golf course. There are scenic walks throughout the 275-acre park, with postcard-perfect views from many spots. The trail out to **Land's End** starts outside the Palace of the Legion of Honor, at the end of El Camino del Mar. Be careful if you hike here; landslides are frequent. *Entrance at 34th Ave. at Clement St.*

⑤ OCEAN BEACH. Stretching 3 mi along the western side of the city, this is a good beach for walking, running, or lying in the sun—but not for swimming. Surfers here wear wet suits year-round as the water is extremely cold. Riptides are also very dangerous here. Paths on both sides of the Great Highway lead from Lincoln Way to Sloat Boulevard (near the zoo). *Along the Great Hwy. from the Cliff House to Sloat Blvd. and beyond.*

⑥ SAN FRANCISCO ZOO. More than 1,000 birds and animals—220 species altogether—reside at the zoo. Among the more than 130 endangered species are the snow leopard, Sumatran tiger, jaguar, and Asian elephant. A favorite attraction is the greater one-horned rhinoceros, next to the African elephants. Another popular resident is Prince Charles, a rare white tiger and the first of its kind to be exhibited in the West. **Gorilla World** is one of the largest and most natural gorilla habitats of any zoo in the world. Fifteen species of rare monkeys—including colobus monkeys, white ruffed lemurs, and macaques—live and play at the two-tier **Primate Discovery Center.** Magellanic penguins waddle about **Penguin Island**; feeding time is 3 PM. Koalas peer out from among the trees in **Koala Crossing,** and kangaroos and wallabies headline the **Walkabout** exhibit. The 7-acre **Puente al Sur** (Bridge to the South) re-creates habitats in South America, replete with a giant anteater, tapir, and a capybaras. The **Feline Conservation Center** is a natural setting for rare cats. Don't miss the big-cat feeding at the **Lion House** Tuesday–Sunday at 2. The **children's zoo** has a population of about 300 mammals, birds, and reptiles, plus an insect zoo, a baby-animal nursery, a deer park, a nature trail, a nature theater, and a restored 1921 Dentzel carousel. *Sloat Blvd. and 45th Ave. (Muni L-Taraval streetcar from downtown), tel. 415/753–7080, www.sfzoo.org. $9 ($1 off with Muni transfer), free 1st Wed. of month. Daily 10–5; children's zoo weekdays 11–4, weekends 10:30–4:30.*

③ SUTRO HEIGHTS PARK. Crows and other large birds battle the heady breezes at this cliff-top park on what were the grounds of the home of former San Francisco mayor Adolph Sutro. All that remains of the main house is its foundation. Climb up for a sweeping view of the Pacific Ocean and the Cliff House below, and try to imagine what the perspective might have been like from one of the upper floors. *Point Lobos and 48th Aves.*

MISSION DISTRICT

The sunny Mission district wins out in San Francisco's system of microclimates—it's always the last to succumb to fog. Home to Italian and Irish communities in the early 20th century, the Mission became heavily Latino in the late 1960s, when immigrants from Mexico and Central America began arriving. Despite its distinctive Latino flavor, in the 1980s and early 1990s the Mission saw an influx of Chinese, Vietnamese, Arabic, and other immigrants, along with a young bohemian crowd enticed by cheap rents and the burgeoning arts-and-entertainment scene. The Mission, still a bit scruffy in patches, lacks some of the glamour of other neighborhoods, but a walk through it provides the opportunity to mix with a heady cross section of San Franciscans.

Numbers in the text correspond to numbers in the margin and on the Mission District/Noe Valley map.

What to See

4 **BALMY ALLEY.** Mission District artists have transformed the walls of their neighborhood with paintings. Balmy Alley is one of the best-executed examples. The entire one-block alley is filled with murals. Local children working with adults started the project in 1971. *24th St. between and parallel to Harrison and Treat Sts. (alley runs south to 25th St.).*

2 **CREATIVITY EXPLORED.** An atmosphere of joyous, if chaotic, creativity pervades the workshops of Creativity Explored, an art education center and gallery for developmentally disabled adults. On weekdays, you can drop by and see the artists at work. 3245

16th St., tel. 415/863–2108, www.creativityexplored.org. Free. Weekdays 9–4, Sat. 11–6.

6 GALERÍA DE LA RAZA/STUDIO 24. San Francisco's premiere showcase for Latino art, the gallery exhibits the works of local and international artists. Next door is the nonprofit Studio 24, which sells prints and paintings by Chicano artists, as well as folk art, mainly from Mexico. 2857 24th St., at Bryant St., tel. 415/826–8009. Wed.–Sun. noon–6.

1 MISSION DOLORES. Mission Dolores encompasses two churches standing side by side. Completed in 1791, the small adobe building known as Mission San Francisco de Asís is the oldest standing structure in San Francisco and the sixth of the 21 California missions founded by Father Junípero Serra in the 18th and early 19th centuries. There is a small museum, and the pretty little mission cemetery (made famous by a scene in Alfred Hitchcock's *Vertigo*) maintains the graves of mid-19th-century European immigrants. Services are held in both the Mission San Francisco de Asís and next door in the handsome multidome basilica. Dolores and 16th Sts., tel. 415/621–8203. Free (donations welcome), audio tour $7. Daily 9–4.

5 PRECITA EYES MURAL ARTS AND VISITORS CENTER. This nonprofit arts organization sponsors guided walks of the Mission District's murals. The bike and walking trips, which take between one and three hours, pass by several dozen murals. Bike tours depart from the **Precita Eyes Mural Center** (348 Precita Ave.); 11 AM walking tours meet at Cafe Venice at 24th and Mission streets. 2981 24th St., tel. 415/285–2287. Center free, tours $8–$10. Center weekdays 10–5, Sat. 10–4, Sun. noon–4; walks weekends at 11 and 1:30 or by appointment; bike tours 2nd Sun. of month at 11.

3 WOMEN'S BUILDING. The cornerstone of the female-owned and -run businesses in the neighborhood is the Women's Building, which since 1979 has held workshops and conferences of particular interest to women. The building's two-sided exterior mural

the mission district/noe valley

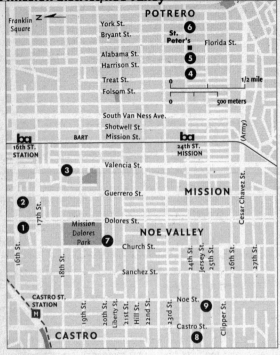

Franklin Square

Z

POTRERO

York St.
Bryant St.

St. Peter's ⑥
Florida St.
⑤

Alabama St.
Harrison St.

④

Treat St.
Folsom St.

0 ········· 1/2 mile

0 ········· 500 meters

South Van Ness Ave.
Shotwell St.
BART
Mission St.

16th ST. STATION

24th ST. MISSION

(Army)

Valencia St.

③

MISSION

Guerrero St.

②

Dolores St.

①

NOE VALLEY

Mission Dolores Park

Church St.

⑦

16th St.

17th St.

18th St.

Sanchez St.

24th St.
Jersey St.
25th St.
26th St.
27th St.

Cesar Chavez St.

CASTRO ST. STATION
Ⓜ

19th St.
20th St.
Liberty St.
21st St.
Hill St.
22nd St.
23rd St.

Noe St.
⑨

Clipper St.

CASTRO

Castro St.
⑧

Axford House, 9

Balmy Alley, 4

Creativity
Explored, 2

Galería de la
Raza/Studio 24, 6

Golden fire
hydrant, 7

Mission Dolores, 1

Noe Valley Branch
Library, 8

Precita Eyes
Mural Arts and
Visitors Center, 5

Women's
Building, 3

depicts women's peacekeeping efforts over the centuries. *3543 18th St., tel. 415/431–1180. Weekdays 9–5.*

NOE VALLEY

Noe Valley and adjacent Twin Peaks were once known as Rancho San Miguel, a parcel of land given to the last Mexican mayor of San Francisco (then known as Yerba Buena) in 1845. Mayor Don José de Jesús Noe built his ranch house at 22nd and Eureka streets, and the area continued as a bucolic farming community until 1906. Because Noe Valley was so little affected by the quake, many of the displaced headed here and decided to stay. It was predominantly working class and largely Irish until the 1970s, when it saw an influx of well-heeled liberals.

Numbers in the text correspond to numbers in the margin and on the Mission District/Noe Valley map.

What to See

❾ AXFORD HOUSE. This mauve house was built in 1877, when Noe Valley was still a rural area, as evidenced by the hayloft in the gable of the adjacent carriage house. The house is perched a few feet above the sidewalk. Several types of roses grow in the well-maintained garden that surrounds the house. *1190 Noe St., at 25th St.*

❼ GOLDEN FIRE HYDRANT. When all the other fire hydrants went dry during the fire that followed the 1906 earthquake, this one kept pumping. Noe Valley and the Mission District were thus spared the devastation wrought elsewhere in the city, which explains the goodly number of prequake homes here. *Church and 20th Sts., southeast corner, across from Mission Dolores Park.*

❽ NOE VALLEY BRANCH LIBRARY. In the early 20th century philanthropist Andrew Carnegie told Americans he would build them elegant libraries if they would fill them with books. A community garden flanks part of the yellow-brick library Carnegie financed, and there's a deck where you can relax and admire

Carnegie's inspired structure. *451 Jersey St., tel. 415/695–5095. Tues. 10–9, Wed. 1–9, Thurs. and Sat. 10–6, Fri. 1–6.*

THE CASTRO

The Castro district is one of the liveliest and most welcoming neighborhoods in the city, especially on weekends. Come weekend, the streets teem with folks out shopping, pushing political causes, heading to art films, and lingering in bars and cafés. Cutting-edge clothing stores and gift shops predominate, and pairs of all genders and sexual persuasions (even heterosexual) hold hands.

Numbers in the text correspond to numbers in the margin and on the Castro and the Haight map.

What to See

★ ❷ **CASTRO THEATRE.** The neon marquee is the neighborhood's great landmark, and the 1,500-seat theater, which opened in 1922, is the grandest of San Francisco's few remaining movie palaces. Before many shows the theater's pipe organ rises from the orchestra pit and an organist plays pop and movie tunes, usually ending with the Jeanette McDonald standard "San Francisco" (go ahead, sing along). *429 Castro St., tel. 415/621–6120.*

❸ **CLARKE'S MANSION.** Built for attorney Alfred "Nobby" Clarke, this off-white baroque Queen Anne home completed in 1892 was dubbed Clarke's Folly when his wife refused to inhabit it because it was in an unfashionable part of town—at the time, everyone who was anyone lived on Nob Hill. *250 Douglass St., between 18th and 19th Sts.*

❶ **HARVEY MILK PLAZA.** An 18-ft-long rainbow flag, a gay icon, flies above this plaza named for the man who electrified the city in 1977 by being elected to its Board of Supervisors as an openly gay candidate. The liberal Milk hadn't served a full year of his term before he and Mayor George Moscone, also a liberal, were shot in November 1978 at City Hall. The gay community became enraged when the famous "Twinkie defense"—that junk food had led to diminished mental capacity—resulted in a manslaughter verdict for the killer. During the so-called White Night Riot of May 21, 1979, gays and their sympathizers stormed City Hall, torching its lobby and several police cars. *Southwest corner of Castro and Market Sts.*

④ RANDALL MUSEUM. The highlight of this facility is the educational animal room, popular with children, where you can observe birds, lizards, snakes, spiders, and other creatures that cannot be released to the wild because of injury or other problems. *199 Museum Way, off Roosevelt Way, tel. 415/554-9600, www.randallmuseum.org. Free. Tues.–Sat. 10–5.*

THE HAIGHT

Once an enclave of large middle-class families of European immigrants, the Haight began to change during the late 1950s and early 1960s. Families were fleeing to the suburbs, and the big old Victorians were deteriorating or being chopped up into cheap housing. Young people found the neighborhood an affordable spot in which they could live according to new precepts. By 1966 the Haight had become a hot spot for rock bands such as the Grateful Dead—whose members moved into a big Victorian near the corner of Haight and Ashbury streets—and Jefferson Airplane, whose grand mansion was north of the district at 2400 Fulton Street.

Numbers in the text correspond to numbers in the margin and on the Castro and the Haight map.

What to See

⑤ BUENA VISTA PARK. Great city views can be had from this eucalyptus-filled park. Although it's not exactly sedate (drug deals are common), it's a very pretty park, especially on a sunny day. Don't wander here after dark. *Haight St. between Lyon St. and Buena Vista Ave. W.*

the castro and the haight

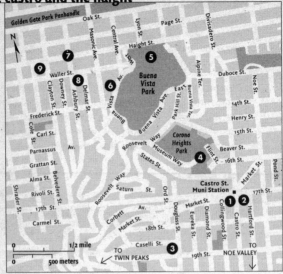

8 GRATEFUL DEAD HOUSE. Nothing unusual marks the house of legend. On the outside, it's just one more well-kept Victorian on a street that's full of them—but true fans of the Dead may find some inspiration here. *710 Ashbury St., just past Waller St.*

7 HAIGHT-ASHBURY INTERSECTION. On October 6, 1967, hippies took over the intersection of Haight and Ashbury streets to proclaim the "Death of Hip." If they thought hip was dead then, they'd find absolute confirmation of it today, what with the Gap holding court on one quadrant of the famed corner. Among the folks who hung out in or near the Haight during the late 1960s were writers Richard Brautigan, Allen Ginsberg, Ken Kesey, and Gary Snyder; anarchist Abbie Hoffman; rock performers Marty Balin, Jerry Garcia, Janis Joplin, and Grace Slick; LSD champion Timothy Leary; and filmmaker Kenneth Anger.

⑨ RED VICTORIAN PEACE CENTER BED & BREAKFAST. In 1977 Sami Sunchild acquired the Red Vic, built as a hotel in 1904, with the aim of preserving the best of 1960s ideals. She decorated her rooms with 1960s themes—one chamber is called the Flower Child Room—and on the ground floor opened the Peace Art Center. Here you can buy her paintings, T-shirts, and "meditative art." *1665 Haight St., tel. 415/864–1978, www.redvic.com.*

⑥ SPRECKELS MANSION. Not to be confused with the Spreckels Mansion of Pacific Heights, this house was built for sugar baron Richard Spreckels in 1887. Later tenants included Jack London and Ambrose Bierce. *737 Buena Vista Ave. W.*

In This Chapter

By Sharon Silva

eating out

SAN FRANCISCO HAS MORE RESTAURANTS per capita than any other city in the United States, and nearly every ethnic cuisine is represented, from Afghan to Indian to Vietnamese. Whether it's the best tapas this side of Barcelona or the silkiest seared foie gras this side of Paris, San Francisco has it all—most often within convenient walking distance.

CATEGORY	COST*
$$$$	over $50
$$$	$30–$50
$$	$20–$30
$	under $20

Per person for a main course at dinner, excluding drinks, service, and sales tax.

THE CASTRO
Contemporary

$–$$$ **MECCA.** This sleek bar and restaurant on the edge of the Castro is a mecca for both local Armani-clad cocktailers and Bay Area foodies. If clubbing is not your thing, reserve a seat in the dining area, away from the always-jammed, velvet-curtained circular bar that anchors the cavernous space. The American menu has an Asian accent. Choices include Korean-style barbecued squid, steamed pork dumplings, crisp roast chicken, and a luscious

downtown san francisco dining

Map of downtown San Francisco dining locations with numbered markers and street labels including North Point St, Francisco St, Chestnut St, Lombard St, Greenwich St, Filbert St, Union St, Green St, Vallejo St, Broadway Tunnel, Pacific Ave, Jackson St, Washington St, Clay St, Sacramento St, California St, Pine St, Bush St, Sutter St, Post St, Geary St, O'Farrell St, Ellis St, Eddy St, Turk St, Golden Gate Ave, McAllister St, Fulton St, Grove St, Hayes St, Market St, Howard St. Neighborhoods: RUSSIAN HILL, NOB HILL, NORTH BEACH, CIVIC CENTER. Cross streets: Scott St, Pierce St, Steiner St, Fillmore St, Webster St, Buchanan St, Laguna St, Octavia St, Gough St, Franklin St, Van Ness Ave, Polk St, Larkin St, Hyde St, Leavenworth St, Jones St, Taylor St, Mason St, Disvisadero St.

blueberry tart. 2029 Market St., tel. 415/621–7000. AE, DC, MC, V. No lunch.

$–$$ 2223. Opened in the mid-1990s, when the Castro was a dining-out wasteland, the smart, sophisticated 2223—the address became the name when the principals couldn't come up with a better one—was an instant success and has continued to attract a loyal clientele. That means you'll need a strong pair of lungs, however, as the restaurant's popularity and absence of sound buffers make conversation difficult. Fried calamari salad, such thin-crust pizzas as French butter and Gorgonzola, assorted dim sum dumplings, and grilled superthick pork chops with sautéed apples and yams are among the kitchen's popular dishes. 2223 Market St., tel. 415/431–0692. AE, DC, MC, V. No lunch weekdays.

CHINATOWN
Chinese

$–$$ GREAT EASTERN. Cantonese chefs are known for their expertise with seafood, and the kitchen at Great Eastern lives up to that venerable tradition. In the busy dining room, large tanks are filled with Dungeness crabs, black bass, abalone, catfish, shrimp, rock cod, and other creatures of the sea, and a wall-hung menu in both Chinese and English specifies the cost of selecting what can be pricey indulgences. Sea conch stir-fried with yellow chives, crab with vermicelli in a clay pot, and steamed fresh scallops with garlic sauce are among the chef's many specialties. In the wee hours Chinese night owls often drop in for a plate of noodles or a bowl of congee (rice gruel). 649 Jackson St., tel. 415/986–2550. AE, MC, V.

$–$$ R&G LOUNGE. The name conjures up an image of a dark bar with a cigarette-smoking piano player, but the restaurant, on two floors, is actually as bright as a new penny. Downstairs (entrance on Kearny Street) is a no-tablecloth dining room that is always packed at lunch and dinner. The classier upstairs space (entrance on Commercial Street), complete with shoji-lined private rooms, is a favorite stop for Chinese businessmen on expense accounts and anyone else seeking exceptional Cantonese banquet fare. A menu with photographs helps diners decide among the many wonderful dishes, from pea shoots stir-fried with garlic to shrimp-stuffed bean curd to deep-fried salt-and-pepper Dungeness crab. *631 Kearny St., tel. 415/982–7877 or 415/982–3811. AE, DC, MC, V.*

CIVIC CENTER
Contemporary

$$–$$$ JARDINIÈRE. One of the city's most talked-about restaurants ★ since its opening in the late 1990s, Jardinière continues to be the place to dine before a performance at the nearby Opera House and Davies Symphony Hall or any time you have something to celebrate. The chef-owner is Traci Des Jardins, and the sophisticated interior, with its eye-catching oval atrium and curving staircase, is the work of designer Pat Kuleto. First courses of sweetbreads and foie gras are pricey but memorable ways to launch any repast. For a more European finish to your meal, you can choose something from the temperature-controlled cheese room in lieu of a dessert-menu item. *300 Grove St., tel. 415/861–5555. Reservations essential. AE, DC, MC, V. No lunch.*

$–$$ CARTA. Although it opened occupying only a single storefront, Carta has expanded into the space next door to create a warm, lavish dining room and comfy bar. The seasonal Mediterranean menu includes a set list of dishes for three months at a time. There is an additional menu of special small and large plates that changes every three weeks. *1772 Market St., tel. 415/863–3516. AE, DC, MC, V. No lunch Sat.*

Mediterranean

$–$$ ZUNI CAFÉ & GRILL. Zuni's Italian-Mediterranean menu and ★ unpretentious atmosphere pack in an eclectic crowd from early morning to late evening. A spacious, window-filled balcony dining area overlooks the large zinc bar, where shellfish, one of the best oyster selections in town, and drinks are dispensed. A whole roast chicken and Tuscan bread salad for two is a popular order here, but don't overlook the generally excellent selection of fresh fish, the grilled rabbit, or the salad of seared chicken livers. Even the hamburgers have an Italian accent—they're topped with Gorgonzola and served on herbed focaccia. The kitchen's shoestring potatoes are addictive, and the coffee granita swirled with cream is pure heaven. *1658 Market St., tel. 415/552-2522. Reservations essential. AE, MC, V. Closed Mon.*

Seafood

$-$$ HAYES STREET GRILL. More than a dozen kinds of seafood are chalked on the blackboard each night at this bustling restaurant. The fish is simply grilled, with a choice of sauces ranging from tomato salsa to a spicy Sichuan peanut concoction to beurre blanc. Fresh crab slaw and superb crab cakes are regular appetizers, and for dessert, the crème brûlée is legendary. *320 Hayes St., tel. 415/863-5545. Reservations essential. AE, D, DC, MC, V. No lunch weekends.*

Vegetarian

$ MILLENNIUM. Tucked into the former carriage house of the venerable Abigail Hotel, Millennium has a menu of "animal-free" dishes made with organic ingredients that keep vegans and their carnivore friends equally satisfied. Try the Caribbean pumpkin curry or steak in marsala sauce, made with seitan, a whole wheat meat substitute. *246 McAllister St., tel. 415/487-9800. MC, V. No lunch.*

COW HOLLOW/MARINA
French

$ BISTRO AIX. This lively bistro is a comfortable space composed of light wood banquettes, paper-top tablecloths, and a heated patio. The friendly service and attractive prices draw diners from the surrounding neighborhood and beyond. On weekdays, an early-bird two-course prix-fixe dinner is available for not much more than the price of a movie ticket. Addictive cracker-crust pizzas, superb steamed mussels, and crisp-skinned roast chicken are additional draws. *3340 Steiner St., tel. 415/202–0100. MC, V. No lunch.*

$ CASSIS BISTRO. Take a seat at the tiny bar and enjoy a glass of wine while you wait for a free table in this sunny yellow, postage stamp–size operation that recalls the small bistros tucked away on side streets in French seaside towns. The servers have solid Gallic accents; the food—onion tart, veal ragout, braised rabbit, tarte Tatin—is comfortingly home style; and the prices are geared toward the penurious. Bare hardwood floors make conversations a challenge on busy nights. *2120 Greenwich St., tel. 415/292–0770. No credit cards. Closed Sun. and Mon. No lunch.*

Italian

$–$$ PANE E VINO. A long table topped with prosciutto, a wheel of Parmigiano-Reggiano, and various antipasti seduces everyone who enters this very popular trattoria. Polenta with mushrooms, grilled bass, and house-made sausages are among the dishes regulars can't resist. The Italian-born owner-chef concentrates on specialties from Tuscany and the north, dishing them up in a charming room with rustic wooden furniture and colorful pottery. *3011 Steiner St., tel. 415/346–2111. MC, V. No lunch Sun.*

$–$$ ZINZINO. The long, narrow dining space—a study in industrial-chic—at this animated *ristorante* ends in a heated patio that fills up on all but the chilliest nights. The menu is irresistible. Thin pizzas are topped with prosciutto and arugula, eggplant and bread crumbs, or fennel sausage and caramelized onions. Veal Milanese arrives under a salad of arugula, tomatoes, and shards of Parmesan, and a wood-fired half chicken is sometimes paired with polenta. *2355 Chestnut St., tel. 415/346–6623. MC, V. No lunch.*

Mediterranean

$–$$ PLUMPJACK CAFÉ. This clubby dining room, with its smartly attired clientele of bankers and brokers, socialites and society scions, takes its name from an opera composed by famed oil tycoon and music lover Gordon Getty, whose sons are two of the partners here. The regularly changing menu spans the Mediterranean; possible dishes include bruschetta topped with white beans and radicchio, duck confit cassoulet, and monkfish with garlic and smoked bacon. *3127 Fillmore St., tel. 415/463–4755. AE, MC, V. Closed Sun. No lunch Sat.*

Mexican

$ CAFÉ MARIMBA. Fanciful folk art adorns the walls of this colorful Mexican café, where an open kitchen turns out contemporary renditions of regional specialties: silken mole *negro* (sauce of chilies and chocolate) from Oaxaca, served in tamales and other dishes; shrimp prepared with roasted onions and tomatoes in the style of Zihuatanejo; and chicken with a marinade from Yucatán stuffed into an excellent taco. Although the food is treated to many innovative touches, authenticity plays a strong role—even the guacamole is made to order in a *molcajete*, the three-legged lava-rock version of a mortar. Fresh fruit drinks and tangy margaritas are good thirst quenchers. *2317 Chestnut St., tel. 415/776–1506. AE, MC, V. No lunch Mon.*

Pan-Asian

$ BETELNUT. A pan-Asian menu and an adventurous drinks list—with everything from house-brewed rice beer to martinis—draw a steady stream of hip diners to this Union Street landmark. Richly lacquered walls, bamboo ceiling fans, and hand-painted posters create a transporting mood in keeping with the unusual but accessible food. Don't pass up a plate of the tasty stir-fried dried anchovies, chilies, peanuts, garlic, and green onions. *2030 Union St., tel. 415/929–8855. D, DC, MC, V.*

Steak

$–$$ **IZZY'S STEAK & CHOP HOUSE.** Izzy Gomez was a legendary San Francisco saloon keeper, and his namesake eatery carries on the tradition. Here, in this old-fashioned, clamorous spot, you'll find terrific steaks, chops, and seafood plus all the trimmings, from cheesy scalloped potatoes to creamed spinach. A collection of Izzy memorabilia and antique advertising art covers almost every inch of wall space. *3345 Steiner St., tel. 415/563–0487. AE, DC, MC, V. No lunch.*

Vegetarian

$ **GREENS.** Long popular with vegetarians and carnivores alike, this beautiful restaurant with expansive bay views is owned and operated by the Green Gulch Zen Buddhist Center of Marin County. A wide, eclectic, and creative range of meatless meals is served, such as corn crepes with smoked cheese and tomatillo sauce; black bean and jicama salad; thin-crust pizzas; southwestern-inspired savory tarts; a grilled tofu sandwich on potato bread; and house-made pastas. Dinners are à la carte on weeknights, but only a five-course prix fixe dinner is served on Saturday. Sunday brunch is a good time to watch local sailboat owners take out their crafts. *Bldg. A, Fort Mason (enter across Marina Blvd. from Safeway), tel. 415/771–6222. D, MC, V. No lunch Mon., no dinner Sun.*

EMBARCADERO NORTH
American

$–$$ **MACARTHUR PARK.** At happy hour, a sea of suits fills this handsomely renovated pre-1906-earthquake brick warehouse. Much of the crowd stays on for the legendary baby back ribs, but the oak-wood smoker and mesquite grill also turn out a wide variety of other all-American dishes, from steaks to hamburgers to seafood. Cobb, spinach, and Caesar salads will add some greens to your meal, and enthusiasts of the skinny french fry will fill up on what is served here. *607 Front St., tel. 415/398–5700. AE, DC, MC, V. No lunch weekends.*

$ FOG CITY DINER. Arguably one of the sleekest American diners, Fog City has a long, narrow dining room that emulates a luxurious railroad car, with dark wood paneling, huge windows, shiny chrome fixtures, and comfortable booths. The menu is both classic and contemporary and includes burgers, fries, chili dogs, hot fudge sundaes, crab cakes, smoked chicken Waldorf, and quesadillas. The shareable small plates are a fun way to go. *1300 Battery St., tel. 415/982–2000. D, DC, MC, V.*

Chinese

$–$$ HARBOR VILLAGE. At lunchtime, businesspeople looking to impress their clients fill the dining room of this outpost of upmarket Cantonese cooking, all of them enjoying the extraordinary array of dim sum. At dinnertime, fresh seafood from the restaurant's own tanks, crisp Peking duck, and various exotica—bird's nest in supreme broth, shark fin, and crab roe— are among the most popular requests from the loyal customers who regularly fill this 400-seat branch of a Hong Kong establishment. The setting is opulent, with Chinese antiques and teak furnishings; a gallery of private rooms harbors large banquet tables perfect for celebrating any special occasion. *4 Embarcadero Center, tel. 415/781–8833. AE, DC, MC, V.*

French

$$$$ GARY DANKO. At his late-1990s eponymous restaurant, chef
★ Gary Danko delivers the same fine food that won him a 1995 James Beard award as best chef in California during his stint at the city's Ritz-Carlton. He has borrowed the hotel's pricing system, too, pegging the cost of a dinner at the number of courses, from three to six. The plates run the gamut from glazed

oysters with leeks, zucchini pearls, and osetra caviar to pan-seared sturgeon with lentils, braised fennel, and saffron to lemon-herb duck breast with celery root–garlic puree and pears to a truly decadent chocolate soufflé. The look of the wood-paneled, banquette-lined room and the smooth gait of the staff are as high class as the food is. *800 N. Point St., tel. 415/749–2060. Reservations essential. AE, D, DC, MC, V. No lunch.*

$–$$ **PASTIS.** At lunchtime the sunny cement bar and sleek wooden banquettes in this exposed-brick dining room are crowded with workers from nearby offices; they come to fuel up on steamed salmon with celery root or grilled prawns marinated in pastis (anise-flavor liqueur). The evening menu may include a dreamy seared foie gras with *verjuice* (sour grape juice); buttery boned oxtail with *ravigote* sauce (with capers, onions, and herbs); and a thick, juicy veal chop with shallot sauce. Pastis, with its French and Basque plates, is chef-owner Gerald Hirigoyen's popular successor to his SoMa bistro Fringale. *1015 Battery St., tel. 415/391–2555. AE, MC, V. Closed Sun. No lunch Sat.*

Greek

$–$$$ **KOKKARI.** Sophistication is written all over this large and handsome taverna. In its warm and inviting interior, complete with an outsized fireplace, displays of rustic cookware and pottery, and a lively bar, folks sit down to a full menu of sunny Aegean plates. Most savvy diners start off with a trio of dips—eggplant, yogurt and cucumber, *taramasalata* (fish roe pureed with olive oil, lemon, and bread crumbs)—served with freshly baked pita and then move on to such Athenian standards as moussaka, roast octopus salad, and braised lamb shank. For a true island experience, cap off your meal with a cup of thick Greek coffee. *200 Jackson St., tel. 415/981–0983. AE, DC, MC, V. Closed Sun. No lunch Sat.*

EMBARCADERO SOUTH
Contemporary

$$–$$$ **BOULEVARD.** Two of San Francisco's top restaurant talents—chef Nancy Oakes and designer Pat Kuleto—are responsible for this highly successful eatery in one of the city's most magnificent buildings. The setting is the 1889 Audiffred Building, a Parisian look-alike that was one of the few downtown buildings to survive the 1906 earthquake and fire. Oakes's menu is seasonally in flux, but you can always count on her signature juxtaposition of delicacies such as foie gras with homey comfort foods such as spit-roasted molasses-cured pork loin and filet mignon with Yukon Gold potatoes. Save room for one of the dynamite desserts, such as cherry–chocolate chip bread pudding or apple toffee pudding. 1 Mission St., tel. 415/543–6084. Reservations essential. AE, D, DC, MC, V. No lunch weekends.

$$–$$$ **ONE MARKET.** A giant among American chefs, Bradley Ogden gained fame at Campton Place and later at his Lark Creek Inn in Marin County. This huge, bustling brasserie across from the Ferry Building is his popular San Francisco outpost. The handsome two-tier dining room, done in mustard tones, seats 170, and a spacious bar-café serves snacks, including addictive wire-thin onion rings, beginning at noon. Fine—and homey—preparations include braised beef shoulder with green olives, fennel, and marrow bones as well as panettone bread pudding with caramel sauce and brandy sabayon. 1 Market St., tel. 415/777–5577. AE, DC, MC, V. Closed Sun. No lunch Sat.

FINANCIAL DISTRICT
Chinese

$ **YANK SING.** The city's oldest tea house, Yank Sing opened in Chinatown in the late 1950s but moved to the Financial District more than a decade ago. The kitchen prepares 100 varieties of dim sum on a rotating basis, serving some 60 varieties daily. The

Battery Street location seats 300, while the older Stevenson Street site is far smaller, a cozy refuge for neighborhood office workers who fuel up on steamed buns and parchment chicken at lunchtime. The newest space is in the Rincon Center, on the Embarcadero. *427 Battery St., tel. 415/781–1111; 49 Stevenson St., at Market St., tel. 415/541–4949; One Rincon Center, 101 Spear St., tel. 415/957–9300. AE, DC, MC, V. Stevenson St. and Rincon Center branches closed Sat. No dinner.*

Contemporary

$$–$$$ RUBICON. With initial investors such as Robin Williams, Robert De Niro, and Francis Ford Coppola, this sleek, cherrywood-lined restaurant was destined to be a hot spot. Set in a stately stone building dating from 1908, the downstairs dining room has the air of a men's club while the upstairs space has a more ascetic feel. The sophisticated fare—sea scallops with truffled fennel puree; yellowtail ceviche; warm radicchio salad with duck confit; white chocolate cheesecake–is served on both floors to Hollywood big shots, suits from nearby office towers, and San Francisco's glamorous set. *558 Sacramento St., tel. 415/434–4100. AE, DC, MC, V. Closed Sun. No lunch Sat.*

$–$$ CYPRESS CLUB. Although restaurateur John Cunin calls his fashionable spot a "San Francisco brasserie," the term is more descriptive of the food—which pleases the contemporary American palate—than the classy but far-out decor. It could be interpreted as anything from a parody of an ancient temple to a futuristic space bar, with stone mosaic floors, hammered copper arches, wall murals depicting scenes of northern California, yards of curved wood, imposing pillars, and overstuffed velvet upholstery. *500 Jackson St., tel. 415/296–8555. AE, DC, MC, V. No lunch.*

French

$–$$ PLOUF. This sleek spot, handsomely turned out in chrome and the color of the sea, is a gold mine for mussel lovers, with eight generously portioned, reasonably priced preparations from which to choose. Among them are *marinière* (garlic and parsley), apple cider, leeks and cream, and crayfish and tomato. Order a side of fries and that's all most appetites will need. Other main courses run the gamut from steak frites to *bourride* (Provençal fish soup). Plouf is French for "splash," and the appetizers maintain the seaside theme, with raw oysters on the half shell and soft-shell crab among the offerings. *40 Belden Pl., tel. 415/986–6491. AE, MC, V. Closed Sun.*

$ CAFÉ CLAUDE. This standout French bistro is in an alley near the Notre Dame des Victoires Catholic church and the French consulate. The interior design is Parisian, with a zinc bar, old-fashioned banquettes, and cinema posters that once actually outfitted a bar in the City of Light's 11th arrondissement. Order an *assiette de charcuterie* (plate of assorted meats) or simple beef *daube* (a stew of braised beef, herbs, spices, and vegetables) from the French-speaking staff, and you might forget what country you're in. On Friday and Saturday nights, the boisterous crowds regularly spill out into the alleyway. *7 Claude La., tel. 415/392–3505. AE, DC, MC, V. No dinner Mon.*

Japanese

$–$$$ KYO-YA. Rarely replicated outside Japan, the refined experience of dining in a fine Japanese restaurant has been introduced with extraordinary authenticity at this showplace within the Palace Hotel. In Japan a *kyo-ya* is a nonspecialized restaurant that serves a wide range of food. Here, the range is spectacular, encompassing tempuras, one-pot dishes, deep-fried and grilled meats, and three dozen sushi selections. The lunch menu is more limited than dinner but does include a *shokado*, a sampler of four dishes encased in a lacquer box. *Palace Hotel, 2 New Montgomery St., at Market St., tel. 415/546–5000. AE, D, DC, MC, V. Closed Sun. No lunch Mon. or Sat.*

Seafood

$$–$$$ **AQUA.** This quietly elegant and ultrafashionable spot is among
★ the city's most lauded seafood restaurants—and among the
most expensive. Chef-owner Michael Mina creates contemporary
versions of French, Italian, and American classics. Mussel soufflé
with a Chardonnay sauce; tuna tartare of ahi tuna, pine nuts, pears,
and quail egg in a sesame-oil dressing; and chunks of lobster
alongside lobster-stuffed ravioli are all especially good. 252
*California St., tel. 415/956–9662. Reservations essential. Jacket and tie.
AE, DC, MC, V. Closed Sun. No lunch Sat.*

Spanish

$ **B44.** Tiny Belden Place is a restaurant gold mine, with a cluster
★ of wonderful European eateries. This Spanish addition, with its
spare modern decor, abstract poster art, and open kitchen, draws
locals who love the menu of authentic Catalan tapas and paellas.
Among the superb small plates are white anchovies with pears
and Idiazábal cheese; sherry-scented fish cheeks with garlic,
parsley, and chili; warm octopus with tiny potatoes; and blood
sausage with white beans and aioli. The paellas bring together
such inviting combinations as chicken, rabbit, and mushrooms
or monkfish, squid, shrimp, mussels, and clams. *44 Belden Pl., tel.
415/986–6287. AE, MC, V. Closed Sun. No lunch Sat.*

THE HAIGHT
Contemporary

$$ **EOS RESTAURANT & WINE BAR.** The culinary marriage of
California cuisine and the Asian pantry is the specialty of chef-
owner Arnold Wong, who serves an impressive East-West menu
at this popular spot. Grilled lamb chops are marinated in a red
Thai curry and served with mashed potatoes; hanger steak is
treated to a Korean marinade before it is slapped on the grill;
Alaskan halibut is steamed in sake; and the more familiar tea-

smoked duck is transformed into aromatic oolong tea–smoked chicken. The wine bar next door shelves hundreds of vintages, any of which is available at your table. *901 Cole St., tel. 415/566–3063. Reservations essential. AE, MC, V. No lunch.*

Indian

$ INDIAN OVEN. This handsome, cozy Victorian storefront never lacks for customers. Many of these lovers of subcontinental food come here to order the tandoori specialties—chicken, lamb, breads—but the *sag paneer* (spinach with Indian cheese) and *aloo gobhi* (potatoes and cauliflower with black mustard seeds and other spices) are also excellent. You can start your meal with crisp vegetable *pakoras* (fritters), served with a sprightly tamarind chutney, chased with an Indian beer or a tall, cool glass of fresh lemonade. A complete meal, called a *thali* for the metal plate on which it is served, includes a choice of entrée, plus soup, a curried vegetable, cardamom-scented basmati rice, nan, and chutney. *223 Fillmore St., tel. 415/626–1628. AE, D, DC, MC, V. No lunch.*

Thai

$ ★ THEP PHANOM. The fine Thai food and the lovely interior at this Lower Haight institution keep local food critics and restaurant goers singing its praises. Duck is deliciously prepared in a variety of ways—in a fragrant curry, minced for salad, resting atop a bed of spinach. Other specialties are seafood in various guises, stuffed chicken wings, and fried quail. A number of daily specials supplement the regular menu, and a wonderful mango sorbet is sometimes offered for dessert. *400 Waller St., tel. 415/431–2526. AE, D, DC, MC, V. No lunch.*

JAPANTOWN
Japanese

$ MIFUNE. Thin, brown soba and thick, white udon are the specialties at this North American outpost of an Osaka-based noodle empire.

A line often snakes out the door, but the house-made noodles, served both hot and cold and with more than a score of toppings, are worth the wait. Seating is at rustic wooden tables, where diners can be heard slurping down big bowls of such traditional Japanese combinations as fish cake–crowned udon and *tenzaru* (cold noodles and hot tempura with a gingery dipping sauce) served on lacquer trays. *Japan Center, Kintetsu Bldg., 1737 Post St., tel. 415/922–0337. Reservations not accepted. AE, D, DC, MC, V.*

$ SANPPO. This modestly priced, casual spot has an enormous selection of almost every type of Japanese food: yakis, nabemono dishes, donburi, udon, and soba, not to mention featherlight tempura and sushi. Grilled eel on rice in a lacquer box and a tempting array of small dishes for snacking make Sanppo a favorite of locals and visitors alike. Ask for validated parking at the Japan Center garage. *1702 Post St., tel. 415/346–3486. Reservations not accepted. MC, V.*

LOWER PACIFIC HEIGHTS
French

$–$$ FLORIO. San Franciscans are always ready to fall in love with little French bistros, and this has made Florio a hit. It has all the elements: simple decor reminiscent of a Paris address, excellent roasted chicken, and some reasonably priced French wines. Of course, there's also duck confit, steamed mussels, and steak *pommes frites.* Forgo the pastas, but don't pass up the crème caramel. The room can get noisy, so don't come here hoping for a quiet tête-à-tête. *1915 Fillmore St., tel. 415/775–4300. MC, V. No lunch.*

Italian

$–$$ LAGHI. For many years, Laghi was a much-loved trattoria in the Richmond District, where it was housed in a small storefront with little available parking. In late 1998, chef-owner Gino Laghi moved his estimable operation to this much larger space, complete with open kitchen, big banquettes, and a sleek wine bar. Old customers and new fans quickly flocked here to enjoy the pastas—including pumpkin-filled ravioli with butter and sage—creamy risottos with everything from fiddlehead ferns to truffles and cream; and roasted rabbit and other game. The wine list of Italian labels is reasonably priced. *2101 Sutter St., tel. 415/931–3774. AE, DC, MC, V. No lunch weekends.*

THE MISSION DISTRICT
Cambodian

$ **ANGKOR BOREI.** This Cambodian restaurant deep in the Mission is a modest yet handsome space decorated with lovely Khmer objects. The menu includes a wonderful array of curries, plump spring rolls, and delicate crepes stuffed with vegetables and a smattering of meat and seafood. Chicken threaded onto skewers, grilled, and served with mildly pickled vegetables is a house specialty. Aromatic Thai basil, lemongrass, and softly sizzling chilies lace many of the dishes at this true neighborhood restaurant. *3471 Mission St., tel. 415/550–8417. AE, D, MC, V. No lunch Sun.*

Contemporary

$–$$ **42 DEGREES.** This industrial-style space, with its curving metal staircase and seductive view of the bay, has been a draw since the mid-1990s. The name refers to the latitude on which Provence, Tuscany, and northern Spain lie. The California menu has Mediterranean influences and includes house-made blood sausage and chorizo; osso buco with couscous and green olives; and fettuccine with house-made lamb sausage, garlic, roasted tomatoes, and Tuscan black cabbage. This is a noisy place, so sensitive ears should beware. *235 16th St., tel. 415/777–5558. MC, V. Closed Sun.–Tues. No lunch.*

French

$ FOREIGN CINEMA. The San Francisco Bay Area is known as home to many of the country's most respected independent filmmakers, making this innovative dining spot a surefire hit with local cinemaphiles. In this hip, loftlike space not only can you sit down to orders of pan-seared foie gras, baked artichoke hearts with warm chèvre, duck breast with mixed berries, and rib-eye steak with *pommes frites* and red wine butter, but you can also watch such foreign classics as Fellini's *La Dolce Vita* and Bergman's *The Seventh Seal*, plus a passel of current indie features, projected in the large courtyard. 2534 Mission St., tel. 415/648–7600. MC, V. *Closed Mon. No lunch.*

$ TI COUZ. Big, thin buckwheat crepes just like you find in Brittany are the specialty here, filled with everything from ham and Gruyère cheese to Nutella and banana ice cream. The blue-and-white European-style dining room is always crowded, and diners too hungry to wait for a seat can try for one next door, where the same owners operate a seafood bar with both raw and cooked choices. The best beverage to sip in this Gallic spot is French hard cider served in classic pottery bowls. 3108 16th St., tel. 415/252–7373. MC, V. *Reservations not accepted.*

Italian

$ ★ DELFINA. Although outfitted with benches and chairs that ensure neighborhood chiropractors a supply of new clients, Delfina is always hopping. Indeed, within several months of opening in 1999, success forced chef-owner Craig Stoll to take over a neighboring storefront to accommodate the throngs. The loyal crowd comes for the simple, yet exquisite Italian fare: grilled fresh sardines; halibut riding atop olives and braised fennel; roast pork topped with a scattering of pomegranate seeds and served with potato–celery root gratin; and profiteroles packed with coffee ice cream and dressed with a lavalike chocolate sauce. 3621 18th St., tel. 415/552–4055. MC, V. *No lunch.*

Latin

$ CHARANGA. Cozy and lively, this neighborhood tapas restaurant, named for a Cuban salsa style that relies on flute and violins, serves an eclectic mix of small plates, from mushrooms cooked with garlic and sherry to *patatas bravas* (twice-fried potatoes with a roasted-tomato sauce), to ceviche. Asian influences show up on this Latin table as well, in such dishes as shrimp and calamari with coconut rice and ginger sauce. The small dining room, with its walls of exposed brick and soothing green, is a friendly, fun place to eat and socialize. Order a pitcher of sangria and enjoy yourself. 2351 Mission St., tel. 415/282–1813. *Reservations not accepted. MC, V. Closed Sun. and Mon. No lunch.*

Mexican

$ LA TAQUERIA. Although there are a number of taquerías in the Mission, this attractive spot, with its arched exterior and modest interior, is one of the oldest and finest. The tacos are superb: a pair of warm corn tortillas topped with your choice of meat—*carne asada* (grilled steak) and *carnitas* (slowly cooked pork) are favorites—and a spoonful of perfectly fresh salsa. Big appetites may want to try one of the burritos, a large flour tortilla wrapped around hearty spoonfuls of meat, rice, beans, and salsa. Chase your chili-laced meal with a cooling *agua fresca* (fresh fruit cooler) of watermelon or pineapple. 2889 Mission St., tel. 415/285–7117. *No credit cards.*

Spanish

$ RAMBLAS. You can perch on high stools at bar tables or sit in a comfy booth in the rear and enjoy selections from a menu of some 20 tapas, both hot and cold, including serrano ham; *boquerones* (marinated white anchovies); and grilled squid with lemon, fried almonds, and spinach with pine nuts and raisins. A large wine list includes reds, whites, and sherries by the glass, and there are more than a dozen first-class beers, about half locally brewed and the rest from Belgium. *557 Valencia St., tel. 415/565–0207. Reservations not accepted. MC, V. No lunch Sun.*

Vietnamese

$–$$ SLANTED DOOR. Behind the canted facade of this trendy north Mission restaurant, you'll find what owner Charles Phan describes as "real Vietnamese home cooking." There are fresh spring rolls packed with rice noodles, pork, shrimp, and pungent mint leaves, and fried vegetarian imperial rolls concealing bean thread noodles, cabbage, and taro. Five-spice chicken, green papaya salad, and a special of steamed sea bass fillet are among the most popular dishes. *584 Valencia St., tel. 415/861–8032. MC, V. Closed Mon.*

NOB HILL
French

$$$–$$$$ RITZ-CARLTON DINING ROOM AND TERRACE. There are two
★ distinctly different places to eat in this neoclassic Nob Hill showplace. The Dining Room is formal and elegant and has a harpist playing. It serves only three- to five-course dinners, priced by the number of courses, not by the item. The Terrace, a cheerful, informal spot with a large garden patio for outdoor dining, serves breakfast, lunch, dinner, and a Sunday jazz brunch. In the Dining Room executive chef Sylvain Portay, who was previously chef de cuisine at New York's Le Cirque, turns out an urbane seasonal French menu—squab stuffed with port-marinated figs and preserved lemons; lobster salad with caviar cream; and a dreamy chocolate soufflé. *600 Stockton St., tel. 415/296–7465. AE, D, DC, MC, V. Closed Sun. No lunch.*

NORTH BEACH
Afghan

$ HELMAND. Don't be put off by Helmand's location on a rather scruffy block of Broadway—inside you'll find authentic Afghan cooking, elegant surroundings with white table linens and rich Afghan carpets, and amazingly low prices. Highlights include *aushak* (leek-filled ravioli served with yogurt and ground beef), pumpkin served with yogurt and garlic sauce, and any of the tender lamb dishes. *430 Broadway, tel. 415/362–0641. AE, MC, V. Closed Mon. No lunch.*

Contemporary

$–$$ BLACK CAT. A combination restaurant and jazz lounge—the latter called the Blue Bar—Black Cat proved unlucky in its first life when it was trying to juggle what was essentially four menus: Italian, Chinese, old San Francisco, and seafood. Since its difficult debut in 1997, it has narrowed the focus to mostly contemporary American and classic Chinese. Noodles, rice porridge, dumplings, poultry, and seafood dishes (crab in black bean sauce, for example) make up most of the Asian selection, while salads, chops, steaks, fish, and shellfish are the heart of the Western menu. *501 Broadway, tel. 415/981–2233. AE, DC, MC, V.*

$–$$ ENRICO'S SIDEWALK CAFÉ. For years this historic North Beach hangout was more a drinking spot than a dining destination, but a reliable kitchen has changed all that. Diners regularly tuck into the Caesar salad, thin-crust pizzas, steamed mussels, thick and juicy hamburgers, and nicely tossed pastas and grilled fish while gently swaying to first-rate live music. Grazers will be happy to find a slew of eclectic tapas, from smoked salmon bruschetta to fried oysters. *504 Broadway, tel. 415/982–6223. AE, DC, MC, V.*

$–$$ MOOSE'S. Restaurateur Ed Moose and his wife, Mary Etta, are well known in San Francisco, having run another popular North Beach spot before they opened this high-traffic dining room in the early 1990s. Politicians and media types followed them from their former digs, making celebrity sightings a regular sport here. The menu is a sophisticated take on familiar preparations, such as crab cakes with apple salad and lemon aioli; pan-seared Maine scallops with lobster risotto; and braised veal shanks with sour cream mashed potatoes. The surroundings are classic and comfortable, with views of Washington Square and Russian Hill. *1652 Stockton St., tel. 415/989–7800. Reservations essential. AE, DC, MC, V. No lunch Mon.–Wed.*

Italian

$–$$ ROSE PISTOLA. Chef-owner Reed Hearon's popular 130-seat
★ spot draws huge crowds. The name honors one of North Beach's most revered barkeeps, and the food celebrates the neighborhood's Ligurian roots. A wide assortment of small cold and hot antipasti—roasted peppers, house-cured fish, fava beans, and pecorino cheese—and pizzas from the wood-burning oven are favorites. A large and inviting bar area opens onto the sidewalk, and an immense exhibition kitchen lets you keep an eye on your order. *532 Columbus Ave., tel. 415/399–0499. Reservations essential. AE, DC, MC, V.*

$ L'OSTERIA DEL FORNO. An Italian-speaking staff, a small and unpretentious dining area, and irresistible aromas drifting from the open kitchen make customers who pass through the door of this modest storefront operation feel as if they've just stumbled into Italy. The kitchen produces small plates of simply cooked vegetables, a few baked pastas, a roast of the day, creamy polenta, and wonderful thin-crust pizzas—including a memorable "white" pie topped with porcini mushrooms and mozzarella. *519 Columbus Ave., tel. 415/982–1124. Reservations not accepted. No credit cards. Closed Tues.*

Middle Eastern

$–$$ MAYKADEH. Although it sits in the middle of a decidedly Italian neighborhood, this authentic Persian restaurant serves a large following of faithful customers. Lamb dishes with rice are the specialties, served in a setting so elegant that the modest check comes as a surprise. The chicken, lamb, and beef kabobs and the *chelo* (Persian pilaf) are popular choices. Anyone looking for a hearty, traditional main dish should order *ghorme sabzee*, lamb shank braised with onions, garlic, leeks, red beans, and a bouquet of Middle Eastern spices. *470 Green St., tel. 415/362–8286. MC, V. No lunch Mon.–Thurs.*

NORTHERN WATERFRONT
Seafood

$–$$ MCCORMICK & KULETO'S. This seafood emporium in Ghirardelli Square is a visitor's dream come true: a fabulous view of the bay from every seat in the house; an Old San Francisco atmosphere; and dozens of varieties of fish and shellfish prepared in scores of globe-circling ways, such as quesadillas, pot stickers, fish cakes, grills, pastas, and stew. The food has its ups and downs— stick with the simplest preparations, such as oysters on the half shell and grilled fish—but even on foggy days you can count on the view. *Ghirardelli Sq. at Beach and Larkin Sts., tel. 415/929–1730. AE, D, DC, MC, V.*

RICHMOND DISTRICT
Chinese

$–$$ PARC HONG KONG RESTAURANT. The name has changed and so has the owner, but this upmarket Cantonese restaurant has the same chef and staff that made it a Richmond District legend known for serving such classy plates as smoked black cod and Peking duck. The kitchen is celebrated for its seafood, which is plucked straight from tanks; in the cool months, Dungeness crab and Maine lobster are sometimes priced to sell. Chefs here keep up with whatever is hot in Hong Kong eateries, so check with the generally genial waiters to find out what's new on the menu. *5322 Geary Blvd., tel. 415/668–8998. AE, D, DC, MC, V.*

$–$$ TON KIANG. The lightly seasoned Hakka cuisine of southern
★ China, rarely found in this country, was introduced to San Francisco

When you pack your MCI Calling Card, it's like packing your loved ones along too.

Your MCI Calling Card is the easy way to stay in touch when you travel. Use it to call to and from over 125 countries. Plus, every time you call, you can earn frequent flier miles. So wherever your travels take you, call home with your MCI Calling Card. It's even easy to get one. Just visit **www.mci.com/worldphone**.

EASY TO CALL WORLDWIDE

1. Just enter the WorldPhone® access number of the country you're calling from.
2. Enter or give the operator your MCI Calling Card number.
3. Enter or give the number you're calling.

Argentina	0-800-222-6249
Bermuda ÷	1-800-888-8000
Brazil	000-8012
United States	1-800-888-8000

÷ Limited availability.

EARN FREQUENT FLIER MILES

SEE THE WORLD
IN FULL COLOR

Fodor's Exploring Guides bring all the great sights vividly to life with hundreds of photographs, fascinating historical background, and colorful anecdotes. Detailed maps and practical information keep you headed in the right direction.

Pair a Fodor's Exploring Guide with your trusted Fodor's Pocket Guide for a complete planning package.

Fodor's EXPLORING GUIDES

At bookstores everywhere.

at this restaurant, with such regional specialties as salt-baked chicken, braised stuffed bean curd, delicate fish and beef balls, and various clay pots of meats and seafoods. Don't overlook the other seafood offerings here—salt-and-pepper squid or shrimp, smoked black cod, or stir-fried crab, for example. The dim sum is arguably the finest in the city; especially noteworthy are the dumplings stuffed with shark's fin. 5821 Geary Blvd., tel. 415/387–8273. MC, V.

Japanese

$–$$ KABUTO SUSHI. For one of the most spectacular acts in town, head down Geary Boulevard past Japantown to Kabuto. Here, behind the sushi counter, master chef Sachio Kojima flashes his knives before an admiring crowd who can't get enough of his buttery yellowfin tuna, raw shrimp, or golden sea urchin on pads of pearly rice. In addition to exceptional sushi and sashimi, traditional Japanese dinners are served in the adjoining dining room. For an authentic experience, request tatami seating in the shoji-screened area. Be sure to consider the excellent selection of sakes. 5116 Geary Blvd., tel. 415/752–5652. MC, V. Closed Sun. and Mon. No lunch.

Russian

$ KATIA'S. This bright Richmond District gem serves Russian food with considerable flair at remarkably reasonable prices. Try the borscht, a dollop of sour cream topping a mélange of beets, cabbage, and other vegetables. Small plates of smoked salmon and blini, marinated mushrooms, and meat- or vegetable-filled piroshki are also wonderful ways to start a meal, and light chicken or potato cutlets or delicate pelmeni (small meat-filled dumplings in broth) are fine main courses. Save room for a meringue drizzled with berry sauce or a flaky napoleon. 600 5th Ave., tel. 415/668–9292. AE, D, MC, V. Closed Mon. No lunch weekends.

Singaporean

$ STRAITS CAFÉ. This highly popular restaurant serves the unique fare of Singapore, a cuisine that combines the culinary traditions of China, India, and the Malay archipelago. That mix translates into complex curries, stir-fried seafood, chewy Indian breads, fragrant satays, and seafood noodle soups. The handsome dining room includes one wall that re-creates the old shop-house fronts of Singapore. *3300 Geary Blvd., tel. 415/668–1783.* AE, MC, V.

Vietnamese

$ LE SOLEIL. The food of Vietnam is the specialty of this pastel, light-filled restaurant in the heart of Inner Richmond. An eye-catching painting of Saigon hangs on one wall, and a large aquarium of tropical fish adds to the tranquil mood. The kitchen prepares traditional dishes from every part of the country. Try the excellent raw-beef salad; crisp, flavorful spring rolls; a simple stir-fry of chicken and aromatic fresh basil leaves; or large prawns simmered in a clay pot. *133 Clement St., tel. 415/668–4848.* MC, V.

RUSSIAN HILL
French

$–$$$ ★ LA FOLIE. Long a favorite of dedicated Francophiles, this small, *très* Parisian establishment is a gem. The surroundings are truly lovely, but the food is the real star here, especially the five-course "discovery menu" that allows a sample of such rarified mouthfuls as lobster salad with a mango vinaigrette and quail with white truffles. Much of the food is edible art—whimsical presentations in the form of savory terrines, *galettes* (flat, round cakes), and napoleons—or such elegant accompaniments as bone-marrow flan. The exquisite fare and professional service come at a hefty price, so save this special place for a very special occasion. *2316 Polk St., tel. 415/776–5577. Reservations essential.* AE, D, DC, MC, V. *Closed Sun. No lunch.*

Italian

$$ ACQUERELLO. This elegant restaurant—white tablecloths, fresh flowers, exquisite china—is one of the most romantic spots in town. Both the service and the food are exemplary, and the menu covers the full range of Italian cuisine. The gnocchi and panzarotti are memorable, as are the fish dishes. Chef-owner Suzette Gresham's fine creations include an antipasto of squab paired with favas and borlotti beans, greens, and a main of sautéed sweetbreads with braised artichokes and white wine. *1722 Sacramento St., tel. 415/567–5432. AE, D, MC, V. Closed Sun. and Mon. No lunch.*

Spanish

$ ZARZUELA. Until the mid-'90s San Francisco lacked a great tapas restaurant—but Spanish-born chef Lucas Gasco changed all that when he and partner Andy Debanne opened this charming restaurant. The small, crowded storefront serves nearly 40 different hot and cold tapas plus some dozen main courses. There is a tapa to suit every palate, from poached octopus atop new potatoes and hot garlic-flecked shrimp to slabs of manchego cheese with paper-thin slices of serrano ham. Hop a cable car to get here, as parking is nightmarish. *2000 Hyde St., tel. 415/346–0800. Reservations not accepted. D, MC, V. Closed Sun. and Mon. No lunch.*

Steak

$–$$$ HARRIS'. ★ Ann Harris knows her beef. She grew up on a Texas cattle ranch and was married to the late Jack Harris of Harris Ranch fame. In her own large, New York–style restaurant she serves some of the best dry-aged steaks in town, but don't overlook the starter of spinach salad or the entrée of calves' liver with onions and bacon. Be sure to include a side of the fine creamed spinach. If you're a martini drinker, take this opportunity to enjoy an artful example of the cocktail. *2100 Van Ness Ave., tel. 415/673–1888. AE, D, DC, MC, V. No lunch.*

SOUTH OF MARKET
American

$ MO'S GRILL. The term "burger" takes on new meaning at Mo's, which is within easy walking distance of the Moscone Center and the Museum of Modern Art. This eatery is devoted to what is arguably America's favorite food, and it dresses it up in a variety of ways: with Monterey Jack and avocado; with apple-smoked bacon; with sautéed mushrooms; with cheese and chilies; and more. But beef burgers—freshly ground daily and hand-formed—are not the only story here. Salmon, lamb, and turkey burgers are among the other choices also cooked over the volcanic-rock grill, and sides of fries or onion rings fill out the plates deliciously. 772 Folsom St., tel. 415/957–3779. MC, V.

Contemporary

$$–$$$ FIFTH FLOOR. San Franciscans began fighting for tables at this ★ topflight hotel dining room within days of its opening in 1999; chef George Morrone's elegant, sophisticated, visually stunning plates are the reason why. The 75-seat room is done in dark wood and zebra-stripe carpeting, and such exquisite dishes as roast rack of veal with truffles, suckling pig à l'orange, and medallions of beef and lamb in a pastry crust are served. There's even ice cream made to order—the machine churns out a creamy, cool, rich serving for one. Palomar Hotel, 12 4th St., tel. 415/348–1555. Reservations essential. AE, DC, MC, V. Closed Sun. No lunch.

$$–$$$ HAWTHORNE LANE. In 1995 this high-end establishment on a ★ quiet alley a block or so from the Moscone Center and the Museum of Modern Art opened to great acclaim, and although some of the principals have left, it still deservedly draws a crowd. At the tables in the large, high-ceiling bar, you can order a selection of irresistible small plates—Thai-style squid, skewers of grilled chicken, and tempura-battered green beans with mustard sauce—plus anything on the full menu. Patrons in the somewhat formal, light-flooded dining room engage in more serious eating, from panfried Atlantic salmon to roast rack of veal with black truffles. *22 Hawthorne St., tel. 415/777–9779. Reservations essential. D, DC, MC, V. No lunch weekends.*

French

$–$$ **BIZOU.** Chef Loretta Keller serves a distinctive French country menu at this comfortable corner bistro, the name of which translates as "kiss." Fans of her rustic cooking cite the thin and crisp pizzas, sautéed skate with mashed potatoes, and terrine of duck livers with house-cured pickles as evidence of her talents. The space itself is small and unpretentious. Outsized windows mean it's also sunny and bright. *598 4th St., tel. 415/543–2222. AE, MC, V. Closed Sun. No lunch Sat.*

$–$$ **FRINGALE.** The bright yellow paint on this small, dazzling bistro
★ stands out like a beacon on an otherwise ordinary street. The well-dressed clientele comes for the reasonably priced French-Basque–inspired creations of Biarritz-born chef Gerald Hirigoyen, whose classic *frisées aux lardons* (curly salad greens with crisp bacon cubes and a poached egg), steak frites, duck confit with tiny French lentils, and almond torte filled with custard cream are hallmarks of the regularly changing menu. *570 4th St., tel. 415/ 543–0573. Reservations essential. AE, MC, V. Closed Sun. No lunch Sat.*

$–$$ **SOUTH PARK CAFÉ.** This utterly Parisian spot is open from early morning, for your caffe latte, to late at night, for a wedge of fruit tart or a flute of champagne. No place in the City of Lights itself serves a more authentic steak frites than this warm, sometimes clamorous spot overlooking a grassy square. A notable first-course is the salad greens with baked goat cheese. For an entrée try the duck leg with mashed potatoes or the roast chicken with thin, crisp fries. *108 South Park, at Bryant St., tel. 415/495–7275. MC, V. Closed Sun. No lunch Sat.*

Mediterranean

$–$$ **LULU.** Since its opening day in 1993, a seat at this boisterous
★ restaurant has been one of the hottest tickets in town. The food,
under the watchful eye of executive chef Jody Denton, is satisfyingly
uncomplicated and delectable. Under the high barrel-vaulted
ceiling, beside a large open kitchen, you can feast on sizzling
mussels roasted in an iron skillet; wood-roasted poultry, meats,
and shellfish; plus pizzas and pastas. Sharing dishes is the custom
here. A sister restaurant, Azie, serving a creative fusion menu, is
next door. 816 Folsom St., tel. 415/495–5775. *Reservations essential.*
AE, DC, MC, V.

UNION SQUARE
Contemporary

$$ **POSTRIO.** There's always a chance to catch a glimpse of some
celebrity here, including Postrio's owner, superchef Wolfgang
Puck, who periodically commutes from Los Angeles to make an
appearance in the restaurant's open kitchen. A stunning three-
level bar and dining area is highlighted by palm trees and museum-
quality contemporary paintings. Attire is formal. The food is
Puckish Californian with Mediterranean and Asian overtones—
roast Chinese duck with brown-butter wild rice, house-cured
salmon and caviar on a giant blini—and the desserts, such as dark
chocolate truffle cake with Merlot-poached pears, are irresistible.
There are also substantial breakfast and late-night bar menus (with
great pizzas). 545 Post St., tel. 415/776–7825. *Reservations essential.*
AE, D, DC, MC, V. No lunch Sun.

$–$$ **GRAND CAFÉ.** In the heart of the theater district, this inviting
combination dining room and bar is a magnet for folks seeking
everything from an early morning breakfast to a late-night snack.
The Californian-French menu served in the dining room includes
such crowd pleasers as snapper on a bed of escarole and duck
confit with potato cakes, while the bar serves hearty sandwiches

and thin-crust pizzas. The dramatic and somewhat imposing dining room, formerly a hotel ballroom, has fanciful sculptures of stylized human figures, chandeliers, and eight murals that evoke such early 20th-century styles as expressionism and fauvism. *Hotel Monaco, 501 Geary St., tel. 415/292–0101. AE, D, DC, MC, V.*

$–$$ ORITALIA. For many years, Oritalia—the name is a blend of the Orient and Italy—was a small, highly regarded restaurant in Lower Pacific Heights. In the late 1990s it moved downtown, to a much larger space in the Juliana Hotel. The burnt-orange dining room, with silk-clad chandeliers, ample booths, and carefully chosen Asian artifacts, is a handsome site. The unusual menu includes dishes such as roast chicken with Asian greens served with polenta-stuffed ravioli and sautéed lobster with sweet potato gnocchi. Steamed mussels in coconut sauce and veal carpaccio with ginger-tomato confit are two of the intriguing starters. Desserts are especially imaginative, with luscious creations built from chocolate, caramel, cream, ginger, and other irresistible ingredients. *586 Bush St., tel. 415/782–8122. AE, DC, MC, V. No lunch.*

French

$$$$ MASA'S. Julian Serrano headed up the kitchen at this pretty, flower-filled dining spot in the Vintage Court hotel for more than a dozen years, carrying on the tradition of the restaurant's late founder, Masa Kobayashi. In 1998, the torch was passed to Chad Callahan, who had served as the number two chef for several years. Most regulars agree that Callahan has made this celebrated food temple his own, in a style, although somewhat lightened, that they have come to expect. Dinners are prix fixe, with two menus offered, a four-course menu du jour and a five-course menu, both laced with truffles and foie gras and both priced at a king's ransom. *648 Bush St., tel. 415/989–7154. Reservations essential. Jacket required. AE, D, DC, MC, V. Closed Sun. and Mon. No lunch.*

$$$ FLEUR DE LYS. The creative cooking of French chef-partner Hubert Keller has brought every conceivable culinary award to this romantic spot, which some consider the best French restaurant in town. The menu changes constantly, but such dishes as seared foie gras, sea bass with ratatouille crust, and venison chop with mustard glaze are among the possibilities. Perfectly smooth service adds to the overall enjoyment of eating here. The elaborately canopied dining room is reminiscent of a sheikh's tent. *777 Sutter St., tel. 415/673-7779. Reservations essential. Jacket required. AE, DC, MC, V. Closed Sun. No lunch.*

Italian

$ SCALA'S BISTRO. Smart leather-and-wood booths, an extravagant mural along one wall, and an appealing menu of Italian plates make this one of downtown's most attractive destinations. A large open kitchen stands at the rear of the fashionable dining room, where regulars and out-of-town visitors alike sit down to breakfast, lunch, and dinner. Grilled Portobello mushrooms with greens and a tower of fried calamari or zucchini are among the favorite antipasti, and the pastas and grilled meats are satisfying. *432 Powell St., tel. 415/395-8555. AE, D, DC, MC, V.*

Seafood

$$-$$$ FARALLON. ★ Outfitted with sculpted purple-and-pink jellyfish lamps, kelp-covered columns, sea urchin chandeliers, and seashell covered walls, this swanky Pat Kuleto–designed restaurant is loaded with style *and* customers. Chef Mark Franz, who gained his fame at Stars, cooks up exquisite seafood that draws serious diners from coast to coast. Such showy concoctions as roasted Alaskan char with Tuscan black cabbage and caramelized salsify, and Atlantic cod with fresh Périgord truffles appear on the regularly changing menu. *450 Post St., tel. 415/956-6969. AE, D, DC, MC, V. No lunch Sun. and Mon.*

Vietnamese

$–$$ **LE COLONIAL.** Until the mid-1990s, Trader Vic's, a well-known Polynesian-inspired haunt of the city's social elite, occupied this restaurant. In 1998, Le Colonial refurbished the space—stamped tin ceiling, period photographs, slow-moving fans, tropical plants—creating a 1920s French colonial setting in which to serve its upscale Vietnamese food. The space still draws the local blue bloods, this time for its spring rolls, ribs infused with chili-lime marinade, coconut curry prawns, and other Southeast Asian flavors. Upstairs, a suave lounge with couches is the ideal place to sip a cocktail before dinner. *20 Cosmo Pl., tel. 415/931–3600. AE, MC, V. Closed Sun. No lunch Sat.*

In This Chapter

Updated by Sharron S. Wood

shopping

FROM FRINGE FASHIONS IN THE HAIGHT to leather chaps in the Castro, San Francisco's many distinctive neighborhoods offer consumers a bit of everything. There are ginseng health potions in Chinatown, fine antiques and art in Jackson Square, handmade kimonos in Japantown, and bookstores throughout the city, specializing in everything from Beat poetry to radical politics. For those who prefer the mainstream, there are high-end boutiques on Union Street and fine department stores in Union Square.

MAJOR SHOPPING DISTRICTS
The Castro/Noe Valley

The Castro, often called the gay capital of the world, is also a major shopping destination for nongay travelers. The Castro is filled with men's clothing boutiques, home accessory stores, and various specialty stores. Especially notable is **A DIFFERENT LIGHT,** (489 Castro St., tel. 415/431–0891), one of the country's premier gay and lesbian bookstores. **UNDER ONE ROOF** (549 Castro St., between 18th and 19th Sts., tel. 415/252–9430) donates the profits from its home and garden items, gourmet foods, bath products, books, frames, and cards to northern California AIDS organizations.

Just south of the Castro on 24th Street, largely residential Noe Valley is an enclave of gourmet food stores, used-CD shops, clothing boutiques, and specialty gift stores. At **PANETTI'S** (3927 24th St., between Noe and Sanchez Sts., tel. 415/648–

2414) you'll find offbeat novelty items, whimsical picture frames, journals, and more.

Chinatown

The intersection of Grant Avenue and Bush Street marks the gateway to Chinatown. Here, hordes of shoppers and tourists are introduced to 24 blocks of shops, restaurants, and markets—a nonstop tide of activity. The **GREAT CHINA HERB CO.** (857 Washington St., between Grant Ave. and Stockton St., tel. 415/982–2195), where the bill is tallied on an abacus, is one of the biggest herb stores around.

Embarcadero Center

Five modern towers of shops, restaurants, offices, and a popular movie theater—plus the Hyatt Regency Hotel—make up the Embarcadero Center, downtown at the end of Market Street.

Fisherman's Wharf

A constant throng of sightseers crowds Fisherman's Wharf, and with good reason: Pier 39, the Anchorage, Ghirardelli Square, and the Cannery are all here, each with shops and restaurants, as well as outdoor entertainment—musicians, mimes, and magicians.

The Haight

Haight Street is a perennial attraction for visitors, if only to see the sign at Haight and Ashbury streets—the geographic center of the Flower Power movement during the 1960s. These days chain stores such as the Gap and Ben & Jerry's have taken over large storefronts near the famous intersection, but it's still possible to find high-quality vintage clothing, funky jewelry, folk art from around the world, and used records and CDs galore in this always-busy neighborhood.

Hayes Valley

Hayes Valley, just west of the Civic Center, is packed with art galleries and such unusual stores as **WORLDWARE** (336 Hayes St., between Gough and Franklin Sts., tel. 415/487–9030), where everything from clothing to furniture to candles is made of organic materials.

Jackson Square

Elegant Jackson Square is home to a dozen or so of San Francisco's finest retail antiques dealers, many of which occupy Victorian-era buildings.

Japantown

The **JAPAN CENTER** (between Laguna and Fillmore Sts. and Geary Blvd. and Post St.) is five acres of shopping under one roof. The three-block complex includes an 800-car public garage and three shops-filled buildings. Especially worthwhile are the Kintetsu and Kinokuniya buildings, where shops and showrooms sell electronics, tapes and records, jewelry, antique kimonos, *tansu* chests, paintings, and more.

The Marina District

Chestnut Street, one block north of Lombard Street and stretching from Fillmore to Broderick streets, caters to the shopping whims of Marina District residents, many of whom go for clingy designer clothing and quality housewares.

The Mission

The diverse Mission District, home to a large Latino population, plus young artists and musicians from various nations, draws bargain hunters with its many used-clothing, vintage furniture, and alternative bookstores. Shoppers can unwind with a cup of *café con leche* at one of dozens of cafés.

North Beach

Sometimes compared to New York City's Greenwich Village, North Beach is only a fraction of the size, clustered tightly around Washington Square and Columbus Avenue. Most of its businesses are small eateries, cafés, and shops selling clothing, antiques, and vintage wares. Once the center of the Beat movement, North Beach still has a bohemian spirit that's especially apparent at rambling **CITY LIGHTS BOOKSTORE** (261 Columbus Ave., at Broadway, tel. 415/362–8193), where the Beat poets live on.

Pacific Heights

Pacific Heights residents seeking fine items for their luxurious homes head straight for Fillmore Street between Post Street and Pacific Avenue, and Sacramento Street between Lyon and Maple streets, where private residences alternate with fine clothing and gift shops, housewares stores, and art galleries. A local favorite is the **SUE FISHER KING COMPANY** (3067 Sacramento St., between Baker and Broderick Sts., tel. 415/922–7276), whose quality home accessories fit right into this upscale neighborhood.

South of Market

The semi-industrial zone south of Market, called SoMa, is home to a few discount outlets; most are along the streets and alleyways bordered by 2nd, Townsend, Howard, and 10th streets. At the other end of the spectrum are the high-class gift shops of the **SAN FRANCISCO MUSEUM OF MODERN ART** (151 3rd St., between Mission and Howard Sts., tel. 415/357–4035) and the **CENTER FOR THE ARTS GIFT SHOP** (701 Mission St., at 3rd St., tel. 415/978–2710 Ext. 168). Both sell handmade jewelry and other great gift items.

Union Square

Serious shoppers head straight to Union Square, San Francisco's main shopping area and the site of most department stores, including **MACY'S** (Stockton and O'Farrell Sts., tel. 415/397–3333), **NEIMAN MARCUS** (150 Stockton St., at Geary Blvd., tel. 415/362–3900), and **SAKS FIFTH AVENUE** (384 Post St., at Powell St., tel. 415/986–4300). The **SAN FRANCISCO SHOPPING CENTRE** (865 Market St., between 4th and 5th Sts., tel. 415/495–5656), across from the cable car turnaround at Powell and Market streets, is distinguished by spiral escalators that wind up through the sunlit atrium. Inside are more than 35 retailers. At Post and Kearny streets, the **CROCKER GALLERIA** (50 Post St., tel. 415/393–1505) is a complex of 40 or so mostly upscale shops and restaurants that sit underneath a glass dome.

Union Street

Out-of-towners sometimes confuse Union Street—a popular stretch of shops and restaurants on the north side of the city—with downtown's Union Square. Nestled at the foot of a hill between Pacific Heights and the Marina District, the street is lined with high-end clothing, antiques, and jewelry shops. **UNION STREET GOLDSMITH** (1909 Union St., at Laguna St., tel. 415/776–8048), a local favorite since 1976, prides itself on its wide selection of such rare gemstones as golden sapphires and violet tanzanite.

In This Chapter

Updated by John Andrew Vlahides

outdoor activities and sports

IN SAN FRANCISCO, stockbrokers go swimming at noon, weathered old men brave chilling waters that not even Alcatraz prisoners could swim, and children flock to the Marina Green to fly kites against a backdrop of sailboats. Parks, beaches, and open spaces are as plentiful as bay views and fresh air.

BEACHES

Nestled in a quiet cove between the lush hills adjoining Fort Mason, Ghirardelli Square, and the crowds at Fisherman's Wharf, **AQUATIC PARK** has a tiny, ¼-mi-long sandy beach with gentle water. Keep an eye out for members of the **DOLPHIN CLUB** (tel. 415/441–9329), who come every morning for a dip in these ice-cold waters.

BAKER BEACH is a local favorite, with gorgeous views of the Golden Gate Bridge and the Marin Headlands. Its bold waves make swimming a dangerous prospect, but the mile-long shoreline is ideal for fishing, building sand castles, or watching sea lions play in the surf. On warm days, the entire beach is packed with bodies, including nudists, tanning in the sun.

One of the city's safest swimming beaches, **CHINA BEACH** was named for the poor Chinese fishermen who once camped here. This 600-ft strip of sand, just south of the Presidio, has gentle waters as well as changing rooms, rest rooms, and showers.

South of the Cliff House, **OCEAN BEACH** is certainly not the city's cleanest shore, but its wide, sandy expanse stretches for miles, making it ideal for long walks and runs. You may spot sea lions sunning themselves atop the stony nearby islands. Because of extremely dangerous currents, swimming is not recommended. After the sun sets, bonfires typically form a string of lights along the beach.

PARTICIPANT SPORTS

Due to its natural beauty, physical fitness and outdoor activities are a way of life in the Bay Area. For a listing of running races, tennis tournaments, bicycle races, and other participant sports, check the monthly issues of *City Sports* magazine, available free at sporting goods stores, tennis centers, and other recreational sites.

Bicycling

San Francisco has a number of scenic routes of varied terrain. With its legendary hills, the city offers countless cycling challenges—but also plenty of level ground. To avoid the former, look for a copy of the *San Francisco Biking/Walking Guide* ($2.50) in select bookstores.

The **EMBARCADERO** gives you a clear view of open waters and the Bay Bridge on the pier side and sleek high-rises on the other. Rent a bike ($5 per hour, $25 per day) at **ADVENTURE BICYCLE CO.** (968 Columbus Ave., between Chestnut and Lombard Sts., tel. 415/771–8735). **GOLDEN GATE PARK** is a beautiful maze of roads and hidden bike paths, with rose gardens, lakes, waterfalls, museums, horse stables, bison, and ultimately a spectacular view of the Pacific Ocean. Rent a bike for about $25 per day at **PARK CYCLERY** (1749 Waller St., tel. 415/751–7368). The **MARINA GREEN** is a picturesque lawn stretching along Marina Boulevard, adjacent to Fort Mason. Rent a bike ($5–$7 per hour) at the Lombard branch of **START TO FINISH** (2530 Lombard St., at Divisadero St., tel. 415/202–9830).

Boating and Sailing

San Francisco Bay offers year-round sailing, but tricky currents and strong winds make the bay hazardous for inexperienced navigators.

A DAY ON THE BAY (tel. 415/922–0227) is ideally located in San Francisco's small-craft marina, just minutes from the Golden Gate Bridge and open waters. **CASS' MARINA** (1702 Bridgeway, at Napa St., tel. 415/332–6789), in Sausalito, will rent you any of a variety of 22- to 35-ft sailboats, as long as there's a qualified sailor in your group. **STOW LAKE** (tel. 415/752–0347), in Golden Gate Park, has rowboat, pedal boat, and electric boat rentals.

Fishing

San Franciscans cast lines from the Municipal Pier, Fisherman's Wharf, Baker Beach, or Aquatic Park. **LOVELY MARTHA'S SPORTFISHING** (Fisherman's Wharf, Berth 3, tel. 650/871–1691) offers salmon-fishing excursions as well as bay cruises. **WACKY JACKY** (Fisherman's Wharf, Pier 45, tel. 415/586–9800) will take you salmon fishing in a sleek, fast, and comfortable 50-ft boat. At San Francisco's Lake Merced, you can rent rods and boats, purchase permits and licenses (up to $4 for a permit and $10 for a two-day license) and buy bait at the **LAKE MERCED BOATING & FISHING COMPANY** (1 Harding Rd., tel. 415/681–3310).

Golf

Golfers can putt to their hearts' content in San Francisco. Call the automated **GOLF INFORMATION LINE** (tel. 415/750–4653) to get detailed directions to the city's public golf courses or to reserve a tee time ($1 reservation fee per player) up to seven days in advance. **GLEN EAGLES GOLF COURSE** (2100 Sunnydale Ave., tel. 415/587–2425) is a challenging 9-hole, par-36 course in McLaren Park. **GOLDEN GATE** (47th Ave. between Fulton St. and John F. Kennedy Dr., tel. 415/751–8987) is a 9-hole, par-27 course in Golden Gate Park just above Ocean Beach. **HARDING**

PARK GOLF COURSE (Harding Rd. and Skyline Blvd., tel. 415/ 664–4690) has an 18-hole, par-72 course. **LINCOLN PARK** (34th Ave. and Clement St., tel. 415/221–9911) has an 18-hole, par-68 course. The **PRESIDIO GOLF COURSE** (300 Finley Rd., at Arguello Blvd., tel. 415/561–4661) is an 18-hole, par-72 course managed by Arnold Palmer's company.

Tennis

The San Francisco Recreation and Parks Department maintains 132 public tennis courts throughout the city. The six courts at **MISSION DOLORES PARK** (18th and Dolores Sts.) are available on a first-come, first-served basis. The 21 courts in **GOLDEN GATE PARK** (tel. 415/753–7001) are the only public ones for which you can make advance reservations. Fees range from $5 to $10. For gorgeous views, head up to the steeply sloped **BUENA VISTA PARK** (Buena Vista Ave. and Haight St., tel. 415/ 831–2700). Popular with Marina locals, the four lighted courts at the **MOSCONE RECREATION CENTER** (1800 Chestnut St., at Buchanan St., tel. 415/292–2006) are free but sometimes require a wait. In the southeast corner of the beautiful Presidio, **JULIUS KAHN PLAYGROUND** (W. Pacific Ave., between Spruce and Locust Sts., tel. 415/753–7001) has four free courts.

SPECTATOR SPORTS

For a local perspective on Bay Area sports, look in sports bars and sporting goods stores for the *Bay Sports Review*, which lists game schedules and features interviews with sports luminaries.

Baseball

The **SAN FRANCISCO GIANTS** have moved from their former home, Candlestick (now 3Com) Park, to a new downtown bay-front stadium, Pacific Bell Park (24 Willie Mays Plaza, between 2nd and 3rd Sts., tel. 415/467–8000 or 800/734–4268). To avoid traffic jams, take one of the city buses or Muni lines that run nearby; call **MUNI** (tel. 415/673–6864) for the stop nearest you.

The **OAKLAND A'S** play at the Oakland Coliseum (7000 Coliseum Way, off I–880, north of Hegenberger Rd., Oakland, tel. 510/638–0500). Same-day tickets can usually be purchased at the stadium, but advance purchase is recommended. To reach the Oakland Coliseum, take a BART train to the Coliseum stop.

Basketball

The **GOLDEN STATE WARRIORS** play NBA basketball at the Arena in Oakland (7000 Coliseum Way, off I–880, north of Hegenberger Rd., Oakland, tel. 510/986–2200) from November to April.

Football

The NFC West's **SAN FRANCISCO 49ERS** play at 3Com Park (at Candlestick Point, Jamestown Ave. and Harney Way, tel. 415/656–4900). Tickets are almost always sold out far in advance. The AFC West's **OAKLAND RAIDERS** play at the Oakland Coliseum (7000 Coliseum Way, off I–880, north of Hegenberger Rd., Oakland).

Hockey

Tickets for the NHL's **SAN JOSE SHARKS** are available from **BASS** (tel. 510/762–2277). Games are held at the San Jose Arena.

Soccer

The **SAN JOSE EARTHQUAKES** (1257 S. 10th St., at Alma Dr., San Jose, tel. 408/985–4625) play major-league soccer at Spartan Stadium.

In This Chapter

Updated by Sharron S. Wood

nightlife and the arts

SAN FRANCISCO HAS A TREMENDOUS VARIETY of evening entertainment, from ultrasophisticated piano bars to come-as-you-are dives that reflect the city's gold rush past. Although it's a compact city with the prevailing influences of some neighborhoods spilling into others, the following generalizations should help you find the kind of entertainment you're looking for. **NOB HILL** is noted for its plush piano bars and panoramic skyline lounges. **NORTH BEACH,** infamous for its nude "dance clubs," has cleaned up its image considerably and yet still maintains a sense of its beatnik past in atmospheric bars and coffeehouses. **FISHERMAN'S WHARF,** although touristy, is great for people-watching. Tony **UNION STREET** is home away from home for singles in search of company. South of Market—**SOMA,** for short—has become a hub of nightlife, with a bevy of popular dance clubs, bars, and supper clubs in renovated warehouses and auto shops. The gay and lesbian scenes center around the **CASTRO DISTRICT** and the clubs and bars along **POLK STREET.** Twentysomethings and alternative types should check out the ever-funky **MISSION DISTRICT** and **HAIGHT STREET** scenes.

NIGHTLIFE

Bars generally close between midnight and 2 AM. Bands and other performers usually begin between 8 PM and 11 PM. The cover charge at smaller clubs ranges from $3 to $10. At the larger venues the cover may go up to $30, and tickets can often be purchased through **TICKETS.COM** (tel. 415/776–1999 or 510/

762–2277). For information on who is performing where, check out the *San Francisco Chronicle*'s pink "Datebook" insert—or consult the *San Francisco Bay Guardian*, free and available in racks around the city, listing neighborhood, avant-garde, and budget-priced events. The SF *Weekly* is also free and packed with information on arts events around town. Another handy reference is the weekly magazine *Key*, offered free in most major hotel lobbies.

Cabarets

ASIASF (201 9th St., at Howard St., tel. 415/255–2742) is the hottest place in town for saucy, sexy fun. The entertainment, as well as gracious food service, is provided by "gender illusionists."

CLUB FUGAZI (678 Green St., at Powell St., tel. 415/421–4222) is famous for *Beach Blanket Babylon*, a wacky musical revue that has run since 1974. Although the choreography is colorful, the singers brassy, and the songs witty, the real stars are the comically exotic costumes and famous ceiling-high "hats"—worth the price of admission in themselves. Order tickets as far in advance as possible.

The **MARSH** (1062 Valencia St., near 22nd St., tel. 415/826–5750), in the Mission District, books an eclectic mix of alternative and avant-garde theater, performance art, comedy, and the occasional musical act, with an emphasis on solo performances and seldom-staged plays.

PLUSH ROOM (940 Sutter St., between Leavenworth and Hyde Sts., tel. 415/885–2800), in the York Hotel, is an intimate cabaret space that began in the 1920s as a speakeasy. The luster may have faded a bit, but the 120-seat room still books some excellent talent.

Dance Clubs

EL RIO (3158 Mission St., between Cesar Chavez and Valencia Sts., tel. 415/282–3325) is a casual Mission District spot with open mike Tuesday, flamenco and Latin house music on Wednesday, and live bands on weekends.

HI-BALL LOUNGE (473 Broadway, between Kearny and Montgomery Sts., tel. 415/397–9464), has expanded its offerings beyond the swing bands that made it famous to include live jazz bands and DJs.

METRONOME BALLROOM (1830 17th St., at De Haro St., tel. 415/252–9000), where lessons in all sorts of ballroom dance are given every day, is at its most lively on weekend nights, when ballroom, Latin, and swing dancers come for lessons and revelry.

ROCCAPULCO (3140 Mission St., between Precita and Cesar Chavez Sts., tel. 415/648–6611), a cavernous Mission District Dance hall and restaurant that brings in crowds, has live music and salsa dancing on Friday, Saturday, and Sunday. Occasionally major Latin acts such as Celia Cruz take the stage.

330 RITCH STREET (330 Ritch St., between 3rd and 4th Sts., tel. 415/541–9574), a popular SoMa nightclub, blends a stylish modern look with soul, salsa, and Brit pop sounds.

Jazz

BLUE BAR (591 Broadway, at Columbus Ave., tel. 415/981–2233), tucked beneath the retro Beat-generation restaurant Black Cat, finds thirty- and fortysomethings lounging in funky aqua armchairs around Formica tables.

CAFE DU NORD (2170 Market St., between Church and Sanchez Sts., tel. 415/861–5016) hosts some of the coolest jazz, blues, and alternative sounds in town. The atmosphere in this basement bar could be called "speakeasy hip."

ELBO ROOM (647 Valencia St., between 17th and 18th Sts., tel. 415/552–7788) is a convivial spot to hear up-and-coming jazz acts upstairs, or to relax in the dark, moody bar downstairs.

ENRICO'S (504 Broadway, at Kearny St., tel. 415/982–6223) was the city's hippest North Beach hangout after its 1958 opening.

Today it's hip once again, with an indoor-outdoor café, a fine menu, and mellow nightly jazz combos.

JAZZ AT PEARL'S (256 Columbus Ave., near Broadway, tel. 415/291–8255) is one of the few reminders of North Beach's heady beatnik days. With mostly straight-ahead jazz acts and dim lighting, this club has a mellow feel.

KIMBALL'S EAST (5800 Shellmound St., Emeryville, tel. 510/658–2555), in an East Bay shopping complex just off I–80, hosts such jazz, soul, and R&B talents as Jeffrey Osborne and Mose Allison.

MOOSE'S (1652 Stockton St., near Union St., tel. 415/989–7800), one of North Beach's most popular restaurants, also has great music in its small but stylish bar area.

STORYVILLE (1751 Fulton St., between Central and Masonic Sts., tel. 415/441–1751) is a dressy club showcasing mostly classic jazz and Latin music.

YOSHI'S (510 Embarcadero St., between Washington and Clay Sts., Oakland, tel. 510/238–9200) is one of the area's best jazz venues. Dr. John and Charlie Hunter are just a few of the musicians who play here when they're in town.

Piano Bars

GRAND VIEWS (345 Stockton St., at Sutter St., tel. 415/398–1234), on the top floor of the Grand Hyatt, has piano music and a view of North Beach and the bay.

OVATION (333 Fulton St., near Franklin St., tel. 415/553–8100), in the Inn at the Opera hotel, is a popular spot for a romantic rendezvous.

REDWOOD ROOM (495 Geary St., near Taylor St., tel. 415/775–4700), in the Clift Hotel, is an art deco lounge with a low-key but sensuous ambience.

The **RITZ-CARLTON** (600 Stockton St., at Pine St., tel. 415/296–7465) has a tastefully appointed lobby lounge where a harpist plays during high tea (weekdays 2:30–5, weekends 1–5) and a jazz trio or a pianist plays in the evening.

Rock, Pop, Folk, and Blues

BIMBO'S 365 CLUB (1025 Columbus Ave., at Chestnut St., tel. 415/474–0365) has a plush main room and an adjacent lounge that retain a retro ambience perfect for the "Cocktail Nation" programming that keeps the crowds hopping.

BOTTOM OF THE HILL (1233 17th St., at Texas St., tel. 415/621–4455), in Potrero Hill, showcases some of the city's best local alternative rock. The atmosphere is ultra low-key, although the occasional blockbuster act—Alanis Morissette, Pearl Jam—has been known to hop on stage.

The **FILLMORE** (1805 Geary Blvd., at Fillmore St., tel. 415/346–6000), San Francisco's most famous rock music hall, serves up a varied menu of national and local acts: rock, reggae, grunge, jazz, folk, acid house, and more.

FREIGHT AND SALVAGE COFFEE HOUSE (1111 Addison St., Berkeley, tel. 510/548–1761), one of the finest folk houses in the country, hosts some of the most talented practitioners of folk, blues, Cajun, and bluegrass music.

GREAT AMERICAN MUSIC HALL (859 O'Farrell St., between Polk and Larkin Sts., tel. 415/885–0750) is a great eclectic nightclub. Acts run the gamut from the best in blues, folk, and jazz to alternative rock.

JOHN LEE HOOKER'S BOOM BOOM ROOM (1601 Fillmore St., at Geary Blvd., tel. 415/673–8000) attracts old-timers and hipsters alike with top-notch blues acts and, occasionally, a show by the man himself.

At the **JUSTICE LEAGUE** (628 Divisadero St., near Hayes St., tel. 415/289–2038) you'll find live jazz, hip-hop, funk, and world grooves, as well as DJ-driven dance nights.

LAST DAY SALOON (406 Clement St., between 5th and 6th Aves., tel. 415/387–6343) hosts major entertainers and rising local bands performing blues, Cajun, funk, country, or jazz.

LOU'S PIER 47 (300 Jefferson St., at Jones St., Fisherman's Wharf, tel. 415/771–0377) is the place for jazz, blues, and hot Cajun seafood. Bands typically start playing in the late afternoon and continue until midnight.

PARADISE LOUNGE (1501 Folsom St., at 11th St., tel. 415/621–1912), a quirky lounge with three stages for eclectic live music, DJ events, and dancing, also has beyond-the-fringe performances at the adjoining Transmission Theatre.

PIER 23 (Pier 23, at the Embarcadero, tel. 415/362–5125), a waterfront restaurant by day, turns into a packed club by night, with a musical spectrum ranging from Caribbean and salsa to Motown and reggae.

RED DEVIL LOUNGE (1695 Polk St., at Clay St., tel. 415/921–1695) is a plush supper club where local and up-and-coming funk, rock, and jazz acts perform.

The **SALOON** (1232 Grant Ave., near Columbus Ave., tel. 415/989–7666) is a favorite blues and rock spot among North Beach locals in the know.

SLIM'S (333 11th St., between Harrison and Folsom Sts., tel. 415/522–0333), one of SoMa's most popular nightclubs, specializes in national touring acts—mostly classic rock, blues, jazz, and world music. Co-owner Boz Scaggs helps bring in the crowds and famous headliners.

The **WARFIELD** (982 Market St., at 6th St., tel. 415/775–7722), once a movie palace, is one of the city's largest rock-and-roll venues. Performers range from Porno for Pyros to Suzanne Vega to Harry Connick Jr.

Skyline and Ocean-view Bars

CARNELIAN ROOM (555 California St., at Kearny St., tel. 415/433–7500), on the 52nd floor of the Bank of America Building, has what is perhaps the loftiest view of San Francisco's magnificent skyline. Enjoy dinner or cocktails at 779 ft above the ground.

CITYSCAPE (333 O'Farrell St., at Mason St., tel. 415/771–1400), on the 46th floor of the Hilton Hotel, has dancing until 12:30 or 1 AM.

EQUINOX (5 Embarcadero Center, tel. 415/788–1234), on the 22nd floor of the Hyatt Regency, is known for its revolving 360-degree views of the city.

HARRY DENTON'S STARLIGHT ROOM (450 Powell St., between Post and Sutter Sts., tel. 415/395–8595), on the 21st floor of the Sir Francis Drake Hotel, re-creates the 1950s high life with rose-velvet booths and romantic lighting.

PHINEAS T. BARNACLE (1090 Point Lobos Ave., at the western end of Geary Blvd., tel. 415/666–4016), inside the Cliff House, provides a close-up view of Seal Rock and the Pacific Ocean.

TOP OF THE MARK (999 California St., at Mason St., tel. 415/392–3434), in the Mark Hopkins Inter-Continental, was immortalized by a famous magazine photograph as a hot spot for World War II servicemen on leave or about to ship out.

VIEW LOUNGE (55 4th St., between Mission and Market Sts., tel. 415/896–1600), on the 39th floor of the San Francisco Marriott, has superb views through art deco–influenced windows.

San Francisco's Favorite Bars

BACKFLIP (601 Eddy St., at Larkin St., tel. 415/771–3547), attached to the hipster Phoenix Hotel, is a clubhouse for a space-age rat pack—a combination of aqua-tile retro and Jetsons-attired waitresses and bartenders.

BIX (56 Gold St., off Montgomery St., tel. 415/433–6300), a North Beach institution, is famous for its martinis.

BLONDIES' BAR AND NO GRILL (540 Valencia St., near 16th St., tel. 415/864–2419) has a rare enclosed "smoking lounge" in the back, which makes it a favorite of those who like to light up.

BUENA VISTA CAFÉ (2765 Hyde St., at Beach St., tel. 415/474–5044), the wharf area's most popular bar, introduced Irish coffee to the New World—or so it says.

CYPRESS CLUB (500 Jackson St., at Columbus Ave., tel. 415/296–8555) is an eccentric restaurant-bar where sensual, 1920s-style opulence clashes with Fellini-Dalí frivolity.

At **EDINBURGH CASTLE** (950 Geary St., between Larkin and Polk Sts., tel. 415/885–4074), you can work off your fish-and-chips and Scottish brews with a turn at the dartboard or pool table.

HOUSE OF SHIELDS (39 New Montgomery St., at Market St., tel. 415/392–7732), a saloon-style bar, attracts an older, Financial District crowd after work, when live jazz music is on tap.

SPECS' (12 Saroyan Pl., off Columbus Ave., tel. 415/421–4112), a hidden hangout for artists and poets, is an old-fashioned watering hole reminiscent of the North Beach of days gone by.

The **TONGA ROOM** (950 Mason St., at California St., tel. 415/772–5131), on the Fairmont hotel's terrace level, has fake palm trees, grass huts, and faux monsoons—courtesy of sprinkler-system rain and simulated thunder and lightning.

TOSCA CAFÉ (242 Columbus Ave., near Broadway, tel. 415/391–1244) has an Italian flavor, with opera on the jukebox and an antique espresso machine that's nothing less than a work of art.

VESUVIO CAFÉ (255 Columbus Ave., at Broadway, tel. 415/362–3370) is little altered since its 1960s heyday. The second-floor balcony is a fine vantage point for watching the colorful Broadway-Columbus intersection.

GAY AND LESBIAN NIGHTLIFE
Gay Male Bars

IN THE CASTRO

The **CAFÉ** (2367 Market St., at 17th St., tel. 415/861–3846) is a place where you can chat quietly or dance.

CAFÉ FLORE (2298 Market St., at Noe St., tel. 415/621–8579) attracts a mixed crowd including poets, punks, and poseurs.

The **METRO** (3600 16th St., at Market St., tel. 415/703–9750) is a semi-upscale bar with a balcony overlooking the intersection of Noe, 16th, and Market streets.

MIDNIGHT SUN (4067 18th St., at Castro St., tel. 415/861–4186), one of the Castro's longest-standing and most popular bars, has riotously programmed giant video screens. Don't expect to be able to hear yourself think.

ON/NEAR POLK STREET

The **CINCH** (1723 Polk St., between Washington and Clay Sts., tel. 415/776–4162) is a Wild West–theme neighborhood bar with pinball machines and pool tables.

DIVAS (1002 Post St., at Larkin St., tel. 415/928–6006), in the rough-and-tumble Tenderloin, is the place for transvestites, transsexuals, and their admirers.

KIMO'S (1351 Polk St., at Pine St., tel. 415/885–4535), a laid-back club, has floor-to-ceiling windows that provide a great view of hectic Polk Street.

N TOUCH (1548 Polk St., at Sacramento St., tel. 415/441–8413), a tiny dance bar, has long been popular with Asian–Pacific Islander gay men.

THE SOMA SCENE

Bikers are courted at **EAGLE TAVERN** (398 12th St., at Harrison St., tel. 415/626–0880) with endless drink specials. The Sunday-afternoon "Beer Busts" (3 PM–6 PM) are a social high point and benefit charitable organizations.

The **STUD** (399 9th St., at Harrison St., tel. 415/252–7883) is still going strong seven days a week since its opening in 1966. Each night's music is different—from funk, soul, and hip-hop to '80s tunes to favorites from the glory days of disco.

AROUND TOWN

ESTA NOCHE (3079 16th St., near Valencia St., tel. 415/861–5757), a longtime Mission District establishment, draws a steady crowd of Latino gays, including some of the city's wildest drag queens.

LION PUB (2062 Divisadero St., at Sacramento St., tel. 415/567–6565), one of the community's more established enterprises, is a cozy neighborhood bar with an ever-changing array of antiques.

MARTUNI'S (4 Valencia St., at Market St., tel. 415/241–0205), an elegant, low-key bar at the intersection of the Castro, the Mission, and Hayes Valley, draws a mixed crowd that enjoys cocktails in a refined environment.

Lesbian Bars

CLUB Q (177 Townsend St., at 3rd St., tel. 415/647–8258), a monthly (first Friday of every month) dance party, is the largest lesbian dance event in the Bay Area and is always packed.

KANDY BAR (401 6th St., at Harrison St., tel. 415/337–4962), at SoMa's End Up club, is a weekly show organized by the same people responsible for the long-running Girl Spot. The event features house, hip-hop, and R&B every Saturday from 9 PM.

HOLLYWOOD BILLIARDS (61 Golden Gate Ave., near Taylor St., tel. 415/252–9643), a macho pool hall six nights a week, has become the unlikely host of a smoldering lesbian scene every Wednesday.

The **LEXINGTON CLUB** (3464 19th St., at Lexington St., tel. 415/863–2052) is where, according to its slogan, "Every night is ladies' night."

WILD SIDE WEST (424 Cortland Ave., between Mission and Bayshore Sts., tel. 415/647–3099), though a bit out of the way in Bernal Heights, is a mellow neighborhood hangout where there's always a friendly pool game going on.

THE ARTS

Half-price, same-day tickets to many local and touring stage shows go on sale (cash only) at 11 AM from Tuesday to Saturday at the **TIX BAY AREA** (tel. 415/433–7827) booth, on the Stockton Street side of Union Square, between Geary and Post streets. The city's charge-by-phone ticket service is **TICKETS.COM** (tel. 415/776–1999 or 510/762–2277), with one of its centers in the TIX booth and another at **Wherehouse** (165 Kearny St., at Sutter St., tel. 415/249–0871). **CITY BOX OFFICE** (180 Redwood St., Suite 100, off Van Ness Ave. between Golden Gate Ave. and McAllister St., tel. 415/392–4400) has a charge-by-phone service for many concerts and lectures.

Dance

The **SAN FRANCISCO BALLET** (301 Van Ness Ave., tel. 415/865–2000) has regained much of its luster under artistic director Helgi Tomasson, and both classical and contemporary works have won admiring reviews. Tickets and information are available at the **War Memorial Opera House** (301 Van Ness Ave., tel. 415/865–2000).

The **MARGARET JENKINS DANCE COMPANY** (tel. 415/826–8399) is a nationally acclaimed modern troupe. **SMUIN BALLETS/SF** (tel. 415/665–2222) regularly integrates pop music into its performances. **ODC/SAN FRANCISCO** (tel. 415/863–6606) mounts an annual Yuletide version of *The Velveteen Rabbit* at the Center for the Arts. **JOE GOODE PERFORMANCE GROUP** (tel. 415/648–4848) is known for its physicality and high-flying style.

Film

The **CASTRO THEATRE** (429 Castro St., near Market St., tel. 415/621–6120), designed by art deco master Timothy Pfleuger, is worth visiting for its appearance alone. It hosts revivals as well as foreign and independent engagements.

Across the bay, the spectacular art deco **PARAMOUNT THEATRE** (2025 Broadway, Oakland, near 19th St. BART station, tel. 510/465–6400) alternates between vintage flicks and live performances.

The avant-garde **RED VIC MOVIE HOUSE** (1727 Haight St., between Cole and Shrader Sts., tel. 415/668–3994) screens an adventurous lineup of contemporary and classic American and foreign titles in a funky setting.

The **ROXIE CINEMA** (3117 16th St., between Valencia and Guerrero Sts., tel. 415/863–1087) specializes in film noir and new foreign and indie features.

The **SAN FRANCISCO CINEMATHEQUE** (tel. 415/822–2885) splits its experimental film and video schedule between the **San Francisco Art Institute** (800 Chestnut St., at Jones St., tel. 415/822–2885) and the **Yerba Buena Center for the Arts** (701 Mission St., at 3rd St., tel. 415/978–2787).

Music

SAN FRANCISCO OPERA. Founded in 1923, this world-renowned company has resided in the Civic Center's War Memorial Opera House since it was built in 1932. Over its season, the opera presents approximately 70 performances of 10 operas from September to January and June to July. The box office is at 199 Grove Street, at Van Ness Avenue. *301 Van Ness Ave., at Grove St., tel. 415/864–3330.*

SAN FRANCISCO SYMPHONY. The symphony performs from September to May, with additional summer performances of light classical musical and show tunes. Michael Tilson Thomas, who is known for his innovative programming of 20th-century American works, is the musical director, and he and his orchestra often perform with soloists of the caliber of Andre Watts, Midori, and Bay Area resident Frederica von Stade. Tickets run $12–$100. *Davies Symphony Hall, 201 Van Ness Ave., at Grove St., tel. 415/864–6000.*

Theater

The most venerable commercial theater is the **CURRAN** (445 Geary St., at Mason St., tel. 415/551–2000).

The **GOLDEN GATE** (Golden Gate Ave. at Taylor St., tel. 415/551–2000) is a stylishly refurbished movie theater, now primarily a musical house.

The gorgeously restored 2,500-seat **ORPHEUM** (1192 Market St., at Hyde St., tel. 415/551–2000) is used for the biggest touring shows.

The **AMERICAN CONSERVATORY THEATER (ACT)** is one of the nation's leading regional theaters. The ACT ticket office (tel. 415/749–2228) is at 405 Geary Street. Next door to ACT is its home, the **GEARY THEATER.**

The leading producer of new plays is the **MAGIC THEATRE** (Fort Mason Center, Bldg. D, Laguna St. at Marina Blvd., tel. 415/441–8822).

MARINES MEMORIAL THEATRE (609 Sutter St., at Mason St., tel. 415/771–6900) hosts touring shows plus some local performances.

THEATRE ON THE SQUARE (450 Post St., between Mason and Powell Sts., tel. 415/433–9500) is a popular smaller venue.

For commercial and popular success, nothing beats *Beach Blanket Babylon*, the zany revue that has been running since 1974 at North Beach's **CLUB FUGAZI.**

In This Chapter

Revised by Andy Moore

where to stay

FEW CITIES IN THE UNITED STATES can rival San Francisco's variety in lodging. There are plush hotels ranked among the finest in the world, renovated older buildings with a European flair, and the popular chain hotels found in most American cities. One of the brightest spots in the lodging picture is the proliferation of small bed-and-breakfasts housed in elegant Victorian edifices, where evening hors d'oeuvres and wine service are common practice. Another trend is the growing number of ultradeluxe modern hotels, such as the Radisson Miyako, Hotel Nikko, and the Mandarin Oriental, which specialize in attentive Asian-style hospitality.

San Francisco hotel prices may come as a not-so-pleasant surprise. Weekend rates for double rooms start at about $75 but average about $170 per night citywide. The good news is that discounts are not hard to come by. The **SAN FRANCISCO CONVENTION AND VISITORS BUREAU** (tel. 415/391–2000, www.sfvisitor.org) publishes a free lodging guide with a map and listings of San Francisco and Bay Area hotels. **SAN FRANCISCO RESERVATIONS** (tel. 800/677–1500, www.hotelres.com) handles advance reservations at more than 300 Bay Area hotels.

CATEGORY	COST*
$$$$	over $300
$$$	$210–$300
$$	$120–$210
$	under $120

*All prices are for a standard double room, excluding 14% tax.

UNION SQUARE/DOWNTOWN

$$$$ **CAMPTON PLACE.** Behind a simple brownstone facade with a
★ white awning, in the heart of busy Union Square, quiet reigns.
Highly attentive personal service—from unpacking assistance to
nightly turndown—begins the moment uniformed doormen
greet you outside the marble-floor lobby. Rooms, though a little
smaller than those at other luxury hotels, are supremely elegant,
with pear-wood-accented walls and maple armoires and desks.
Room windows, some with window seats, overlook an atrium,
which creates a cozy, residential feel. *340 Stockton St., 94108, tel.*
415/781–5555 or 800/235–4300, fax 415/955–5536, www.camptonplace.
com. 101 rooms, 9 suites. Restaurant, bar, in-room data ports, in-room
safes, minibars, no-smoking room, room service, gym, dry cleaning,
laundry service, concierge, business services, meeting rooms, parking
(fee). AE, DC, MC, V.

$$$$ **THE CLIFT.** Towering over San Francisco's theater district is the
venerable Clift, scheduled to be transformed in 2001 by Ian
Schrager and Philippe Starck into a "hotel as theater" showplace.
The dramatically designed redwood lobby will have hand-carved
Brazilian cherry and limestone elements and a 20-ft-tall fireplace
with sculpted bronze panels. The renowned Redwood Room is
popular for power breakfasts and, at the end of the working
day, draws an upscale crowd for cocktails and dinner. Guest
rooms are elegant and high-tech, with hand-blown glass lamps,
voluminous silk draperies, colorful throw pillows, and high-speed
Internet access and cordless phones. *495 Geary St., 94102, tel. 415/*
775–4700 or 800/652–5438, fax 415/441–4621, www.clifthotel.com.
293 rooms, 80 suites. 2 restaurants, bar, in-room data ports, in-room
safes, minibars, no-smoking floor, room service, health club, dry cleaning,
laundry service, concierge, business services, meeting rooms, parking
(fee). AE, D, DC, MC, V.

$$$$ **HOTEL NIKKO.** In every Nikko lobby on five continents is a
★ fountain, intended as a gathering place where guests can relax
and socialize. The rooms, some of the most handsome in the city,

have inlaid cherrywood furniture with clean, elegant lines; gold drapes; wheat-color wall coverings; and ingenious window shades, which screen the sun while allowing views of the city. Service throughout the hotel is attentive and sincere, and the staff is multilingual. Don't miss the excellent fifth-floor fitness facility ($6 fee), which has traditional *ofuros* (Japanese soaking tubs), a *kamaburo* (Japanese sauna), and a glass-enclosed swimming pool and whirlpool. Shiatsu massages are also available. *222 Mason St., 94102, tel. 415/394–1111 or 800/645–5687, fax 415/421–0455, www.nikkohotels.com. 510 rooms, 22 suites. Restaurant, bar, sushi bar, in-room data ports, minibars, room service, pool, hair salon, Japanese baths, massage, sauna, gym, dry cleaning, laundry service, concierge, concierge floor, business services, meeting rooms, car rental, parking (fee). AE, D, DC, MC, V.*

$$$$ PAN PACIFIC HOTEL. Exotic flower arrangements and elegant Asian touches set this business-oriented hotel apart from others. A graceful Matisse-inspired bronze sculpture by Elbert Weinberg, *Joie de Danse*, encircles the fountain in the 21-story lobby atrium. Guest rooms, with soft green and beige color schemes and black-and-gold quilted bedspreads with Asian block-print designs, have elegant bathrooms lined with terra-cotta Portuguese marble. Complimentary personal valet service, a "pillow preference program" (the opportunity to choose from a dozen kinds), and a fleet of luxury cars that drop guests at nearby destinations free of charge add up to a pampering experience. *500 Post St., 94102, tel. 415/771–8600 or 800/327–8585, fax 415/398–0267, www.panpac. com. 311 rooms, 19 suites. Restaurant, bar, lobby lounge, in-room data ports, in-room safes, minibars, no-smoking floor, refrigerators, room service, gym, piano, dry cleaning, laundry service, concierge, business services, meeting room, parking (fee). AE, D, DC, MC, V.*

$$$$ PRESCOTT HOTEL. A gourmet's delight might be the best way
★   to describe this plush hotel, thanks to its partnership with Wolfgang Puck's Postrio, one of San Francisco's best restaurants. You can order room service from the restaurant or dine at tables

downtown san francisco lodging

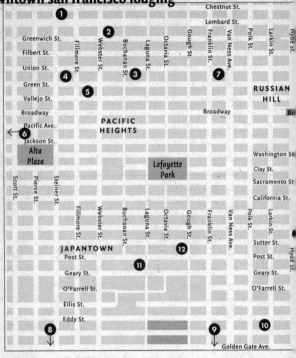

Chestnut St.
Lombard St.
Greenwich St.
Filbert St.
Union St.
Green St.
Vallejo St.
Broadway
Pacific Ave.
Jackson St.

Greenwich St.
Filbert St.
Union St.
Green St.
Vallejo St.
Broadway
Pacific Ave.
Jackson St.

Fillmore St.
Webster St.
Buchanan St.
Laguna St.
Octavia St.
Gough St.
Franklin St.
Van Ness Ave.
Polk St.
Larkin St.
Hyde St.

RUSSIAN HILL

Broadway

PACIFIC HEIGHTS

Alta Plaza

Lafayette Park

Washington St
Clay St.
Sacramento St
California St.

Scott St.
Pierce St.
Steiner St.
Fillmore St.
Webster St.
Buchanan St.
Laguna St.
Octavia St.
Gough St.
Franklin St.
Van Ness Ave.
Polk St.
Larkin St.
Hyde St.

JAPANTOWN
Post St.
Geary St.
O'Farrell St.
Ellis St.
Eddy St.

Sutter St.
Post St.
Geary St.
O'Farrell St.

Golden Gate Ave.

440 yards

400 meters

Chestnut St.

Lombard St.

Greenwich St.

Filbert St.

Union St.

NORTH
BEACH

Columbus Ave.

TELEGRAPH
HILL

San Francisco
Bay

Leavenworth St.

een St.

llejo St.

way Tunnel

cific Ave.

ckson St.

Leavenworth St.

NOB
HILL

Jones St.

Taylor St.

Mason St.

Powell St.

Stockton St.

Grant Ave.

Front St.

Embarcadero

Davis St.

N

Montgomery St.

Sansome St.

Battery St.

Front St.

Davis St.

Drumm St.

CHINATOWN

California St.

Kearny St.

Halleck St.

Steuart St.

Spear St.

ne St.

ush St.

Bush St.

Sutter St.

Maiden
Ln.

UNION
SQUARE

Main St.

Beale St.

Fremont St.

1st St.

New Montgomery St.

2nd St.

Market St.

Mason St.

Taylor St.

5th St.

Mission St.

4th St.

3rd St.

Howard St.

Hawthorne St.

80

is St.

dy St.

Turk St.

reserved for hotel guests—no small perk considering it can otherwise take months to get a reservation at Postrio. The hotel's guest rooms, which vary only in size and shape, have bathrooms with marble-top sinks and gold and pewter fixtures. In the "living room" off the lobby, you can mingle by the fireplace or relax in deep, multicolor leather chairs under a playfully patterned blue-and-gold hand-blown glass window. *545 Post St., 94102, tel. 415/563–0303 or 800/283–7322, fax 415/563–6831, www.prescotthotel.com. 155 rooms, 9 suites. Restaurant, bar, lobby lounge, in-room data ports, minibars, no-smoking floor, room service, gym, concierge, concierge floor, business services, meeting room, parking (fee). AE, D, DC, MC, V.*

$$$$ WESTIN ST. FRANCIS. Since it opened in 1904, illustrious guests of this hotel have included Emperor Hirohito, Queen Elizabeth II, and many U.S. presidents. Its imposing facade, black-marble lobby, and gold-top columns make it look more like a great public building than a hotel; the effect is softened by the columns and exquisite woodwork of its Compass Rose bar and restaurant, a romantic retreat from the bustle of Union Square. Rooms in the modern 32-story tower have Asian-style lacquered furniture; rooms in the original building are smaller but have Empire-style furnishings and retain their Victorian-style moldings. An arcade-level health club (which charges a fee), includes workout facilities, a steam room, and an impressive array of massage services, facials, manicures, and other body treatments. *335 Powell St., 94102, tel. 415/397–7000, fax 415/774–0124, www.westin.com. 1,108 rooms, 84 suites. 3 restaurants, 2 bars, in-room data ports, in-room safes, no-smoking floors, room service, massage, steam room, health club, nightclub, dry cleaning, laundry service, concierge, business services, meeting rooms, travel services, parking (fee). AE, D, DC, MC, V.*

$$$–$$$$ HOTEL MONACO. One of the hippest hotels north of Market ★ Street is the Monaco, with its 1910 yellow beaux-arts facade and plush, eclectically decorated interiors. Inside, past a grand marble staircase, a French inglenook fireplace climbs almost two stories above the lobby toward the three huge domes of a vaulted ceiling hand-painted with hot-air balloons, World War I–era planes, and miles of blue sky. The hotel hosts a complimentary evening wine and appetizer hour, which includes a tarot card reader and massage therapist. Though small, the rooms are comfortable and inviting, with Chinese-inspired armoires, canopy beds, and high-back upholstered chairs. 501 Geary St., 94102, tel. 415/292–0100 or 800/214–4220, fax 415/292–0111, www.monaco-sf.com. 181 rooms, 20 suites. Restaurant, bar, in-room data ports, in-room safes, minibars, no-smoking rooms, room service, massage, spa, dry cleaning, laundry service, business services, parking (fee). AE, D, DC, MC, V.

$$$ **GALLERIA PARK.** Two blocks east of Union Square in the Financial
★ District, this hotel with a black-marble facade is close to the Chinatown Gate and Crocker Galleria, one of San Francisco's most elegant shopping complexes. In the lobby, dominated by a massive hand-sculpted art nouveau fireplace and brightened by a restored 1911 skylight, complimentary coffee and tea are served in the morning, wine in the evening. The third-floor rooftop Cityscape Park has an outdoor jogging track. 191 Sutter St., 94104, tel. 415/781–3060 or 800/792–9639; 800/792–9855 in CA, fax 415/ 433–4409, www.galleriapark.com. 169 rooms, 8 suites. In-room data ports, minibars, no-smoking floor, room service, gym, jogging, dry cleaning, laundry service, concierge, business services, meeting room, parking (fee). AE, D, DC, MC, V.

$$$ **HOTEL REX.** Literary and artistic creativity are celebrated at the
★ stylish Hotel Rex, where thousands of books, largely antiquarian, line the 1920s-style lobby. Original artwork adorns the walls, and the proprietors even host book readings and round-table discussions in the common areas. Upstairs, quotations from works by California writers are painted on the terra-cotta–color walls near the elevator landings. Good-size rooms have writing desks and lamps with whimsically hand-painted shades. Muted check bedspreads, striped carpets, and restored period furnishings

upholstered in deep, rich hues evoke the spirit of 1920s salon society, but rooms also have modern amenities such as voice mail and CD players. 562 Sutter St., 94102, tel. 415/433–4434 or 800/433–4434, fax 415/433–3695, thehotelrex.com. 92 rooms, 2 suites. Bar, lobby lounge, in-room data ports, minibars, no-smoking room, room service, dry cleaning, laundry service, concierge, parking (fee). AE, D, DC, MC, V.

$$$ HOTEL TRITON. This may be the zaniest place to stay in town. You enter via a whimsical lobby of three-leg furniture, star-pattern carpeting, and inverted gilt pillars—stylized spoofs of upside-down Roman columns. The hotel caters to fashion, entertainment, music, and film-industry types, who seem to appreciate the iridescent multicolor rooms with S-curve chairs, curly-neck lamps, and oddball light fixtures. On the downside, rooms are uncommonly small. Twenty-four rooms have been designated environmentally sensitive. They have extra air and water filtration, biodegradable toiletries, and all-natural linens. 342 Grant Ave., 94108, tel. 415/394–0500 or 888/364–2622, fax 415/394–0555, www.hotel-tritonsf.com. 133 rooms, 7 suites. Café, dining room, in-room data ports, minibars, no-smoking floor, room service, gym, dry cleaning, laundry service, business services, meeting room, parking (fee). AE, D, MC, V.

$$$ SIR FRANCIS DRAKE HOTEL. Beefeater-costumed doormen welcome you into the regal lobby of this 1928 landmark property, decked out with boldly striped banners, plush velvet furniture, wrought-iron balustrades, chandeliers, and Italian marble. Harry Denton's Starlight Room, one of the city's plushest skyline bars, is on the top floor. The hotel's surprisingly affordable restaurant, Scala's Bistro, serves excellent food in its dramatic though somewhat noisy bi-level dining room. 450 Powell St., 94102, tel. 415/392–7755 or 800/227–5480, fax 415/391–8719, www.sirfrancisdrake.com. 412 rooms, 5 suites. 2 restaurants, in-room data ports, minibars, no-smoking room, gym, nightclub, dry cleaning, laundry service, concierge, business services, meeting rooms, parking (fee). AE, D, DC, MC, V.

$$$ VINTAGE COURT. This bit of the Napa Valley just off Union Square has inviting rooms—some with sunny window seats—all with large writing desks and big easy chairs. The Wine Country theme extends to the complimentary wine served nightly in front of the lobby fireplace. *650 Bush St., 94108, tel. 415/392–4666 or 800/ 654–1100, fax 415/433–4065, www.vintagecourt.com. 107 rooms, 1 suite. Restaurant, bar, minibars, no-smoking floor, refrigerators, gym, parking (fee). AE, D, DC, MC, V.*

$$–$$$ HOTEL DIVA. A striking black-granite and layered green-glass facade beckons you into the Diva's lobby, where a stylized 1920s ocean liner motif takes over. Nautical touches in the rooms include cobalt-blue carpets and brushed-steel headboards in the shape of ocean waves. Although the Diva's proximity to the Curran Theater attracts actors, musicians, and others of an artistic bent, the hotel is also popular with business travelers, who have free access to the compact business center, and families, who entertain themselves with the in-room Nintendo and VCRs. A complimentary Continental breakfast is delivered to your room. *440 Geary St., 94102, tel. 415/885–0200 or 800/553–1900, fax 415/ 346–6613, www.hoteldiva.com. 88 rooms, 23 suites. Restaurant, in-room data ports, in-room safes, in-room VCRs, minibars, no-smoking floor, room service, gym, dry cleaning, laundry service, concierge, business services, meeting room, parking (fee). AE, D, DC, MC, V.*

$$–$$$ INN AT UNION SQUARE. The tiny but captivating lobby of this small hotel has trompe l'oeil wallpaper depicting a window's "view" of an old town square, making the place feel like a home in some charming, mythical past. The comfortable rooms, some decorated in old-world Georgian style with fireplaces, some in a lighter, more contemporary style, all include nice touches such as goose-down pillows, fresh flowers, and morning newspapers. Bathrooms have attractive granite vanities. You can lounge by the wood-burning fireplaces found in each floor's tiny sitting area, where both complimentary Continental breakfast and evening wine and hors d'oeuvres are served. *440 Post St., 94102, tel. 415/*

397–3510 or 800/288–4346, fax 415/989–0529, www.unionsquare.com. 23 rooms, 7 suites. In-room data ports, no-smoking rooms, massage, parking (fee). AE, DC, MC, V.

$$–$$$ THE MAXWELL. Behind dramatic black-and-red curtains, the Maxwell's lobby makes an impression with boldly patterned furniture in rich velvets and brocades. The hotel is handsome, stylish, and just a block from Union Square. Rooms have a clubby, retro feel, with deep jewel tones and classic Edward Hopper prints on the walls. Baths also sport a retro 1930s look with pedestal sinks and white porcelain faucet handles. Max's on the Square serves American breakfast, lunch, and dinner as well as after-theater dinner and drinks. 386 Geary St., 94102, tel. 415/986–2000 or 888/734–6299, fax 415/397–2447, www.maxwellhotel.com. 150 rooms, 3 suites. Restaurant, bar, in-room data ports, no-smoking room, room service, laundry service, concierge, parking (fee). AE, D, DC, MC, V.

$$–$$$ SHANNON COURT HOTEL. Passing through the elaborate wrought-iron and glass entrance into the marble-tile lobby, with its Spanish-style arches and Oriental carpets, evokes the old-world charm of turn-of-the-20th-century San Francisco. This hotel has some of the most spacious standard rooms in the Union Square area; many have sofa beds for families. Two of the luxury suites on the 16th floor have rooftop terraces with lofty city views. Complimentary morning coffee and afternoon tea and cookies are served in the lobby area. 550 Geary St., 94102, tel. 415/775–5000 or 800/228–8830, fax 415/928–6813, www.shannoncourt.com. 168 rooms, 4 suites. Restaurant, bar, no-smoking floor, refrigerators, dry cleaning, laundry service, concierge, parking (fee). AE, D, DC, MC, V.

$$–$$$ YORK HOTEL. Hitchcock fans may recognize the exterior of this reasonably priced, family-owned hotel four blocks west of Union Square. It's the building where Kim Novak stayed in Vertigo. Inside, the peach-stone facade and ornate, high-ceiling lobby give the hotel a touch of elegance. The moderate-size rooms—all with huge closets—are a tasteful mix of Mediterranean styles, with a terra-cotta, burgundy, and forest-green color scheme. The Plush Room cabaret, where well-known entertainers perform four to five times a week, is the York's drawing card. Continental breakfast is included. 940 Sutter St., 94109, tel. 415/885–6800 or 800/808–9675, fax 415/885–2115, www.yorkhotel.com. 91 rooms, 5 suites. Bar, in-room data ports, in-room safes, minibars, no-smoking floor, gym, nightclub, laundry service, concierge, business services, parking (fee). AE, D, DC, MC, V.

$$ THE ANDREWS. Two blocks west of Union Square, this Queen Anne–style abode with a gold-and-buff facade began its life in 1905 as the Sultan Turkish Baths. Today Victorian antique reproductions, old-fashioned flower curtains with lace sheers, iron bedsteads, and large closets more than make up for the diminutive size of guest rooms (the scrupulously clean bathrooms are even smaller). The buffet-style Continental breakfast, served on each floor, is complimentary. 624 Post St., 94109, tel. 415/563–6877 or 800/926–3739, fax 415/928–6919, www.andrewshotel.com. 48 rooms. Restaurant, no-smoking floor, concierge, parking (fee). AE, DC, MC, V.

$$ CHANCELLOR HOTEL. Built for the 1915 Panama Pacific International Exposition, the Chancellor was the tallest building in San Francisco when it opened. Although not as grand now as some of its neighbors, this busy hotel is one of the best buys on Union Square for visitors wanting comfort without extravagance. Floor-to-ceiling windows in the modest lobby overlook cable cars on Powell Street en route to nearby Union Square or Fisherman's Wharf. The moderate-size Edwardian-style rooms have high ceilings and blue, cream, and rose color schemes; deep bathtubs are a treat. Connecting rooms are available for families, and the Chancellor Café is a handy place for meals. 433 Powell St., 94102, tel. 415/362–2004 or 800/428–4748, fax 415/362–1403, www.chancellorhotel.com. 135 rooms, 2 suites. Restaurant, bar, in-room safes, no-smoking floor, room service, laundry service, concierge, car rental, parking (fee). AE, D, DC, MC, V.

$$ CLARION BEDFORD HOTEL. You'll pass under art nouveau arches carved with grapevines and birds upon entering the bright yellow lobby of this handsome 1929 building. Avant-garde film posters from 1920s Russia adorn the walls. The light and airy rooms have white furniture, canopy beds, and vibrant floral bedspreads. Most rooms in this 17-story hotel (it's the tallest on the block) have gorgeous bay and city views, but the baths are small. Business-class guest rooms have special desk lighting and an ergonomic chair. *761 Post St., 94109, tel. 415/673–6040 or 800/227–5642, fax 415/563–6739, www.hotelbedford.com. 137 rooms, 7 suites. Bar, café, in-room data ports, minibars, room service, dry cleaning, laundry service, parking (fee). AE, D, DC, MC, V.*

$$ COMMODORE INTERNATIONAL. Entering the lobby is like stepping onto the main deck of an ocean liner of yore: neo-deco chairs look like the backdrop for a film about transatlantic crossings; and steps away is the Titanic Café, where goldfish bowls and bathysphere-inspired lights add to the sea-cruise mood. The fairly large rooms with monster closets are painted in soft yellows and golds and display photographs of San Francisco landmarks. If red is your color, you may find yourself glued to a seat in the hotel's Red Room, a startlingly scarlet cocktail lounge filled with well-dressed hipsters. *825 Sutter St., 94109, tel. 415/923–6800 or 800/338–6848, fax 415/923–6804, thecommodorehotel.com. 112 rooms, 1 suite. Restaurant, in-room data ports, no-smoking room, nightclub, dry cleaning, laundry service, concierge, parking (fee). AE, D, MC, V.*

$$ KING GEORGE. The staff at the King George has prided itself on service and hospitality since the hotel's opening in 1914, when guest rooms started at $1 a night. Prices have remained relatively low compared to other hotels in the neighborhood. The front desk and concierge staff are adept at catering to your every whim: they'll book anything from a Fisherman's Wharf tour to a dinner reservation. Rooms are compact but nicely furnished in classic English style, with walnut furniture and a royal-red and green color scheme. High tea at the Windsor Tearoom is an authentic English treat. 334 Mason St., 94102, tel. 415/781–5050 or 800/288–6005, fax 415/391–6976, www.kinggeorge.com. 141 rooms, 1 suite. Tea shop, in-room data ports, in-room safes, no-smoking floor, dry cleaning, laundry service, concierge, business services, meeting room, parking (fee). AE, D, DC, MC, V.

$$ PETITE AUBERGE. The dozens of teddy bears in the reception area may seem a bit precious, but the provincial decor of the rooms in this re-creation of a French country inn never strays past the mark. Rooms are small, and each has a teddy bear, bright flowered wallpaper, an old-fashioned writing desk, and a much-needed armoire—there's little or no closet space. Many rooms have working fireplaces; the suite has a whirlpool tub. Afternoon tea, wine, and hors d'oeuvres are served in the lobby by the fire, and a full breakfast is included. The entire inn is no-smoking. 863 Bush St., 94108, tel. 415/928–6000 or 800/365–3004, fax 415/775–5717, www.foursisters.com. 25 rooms, 1 suite. Breakfast room, parking (fee). AE, DC, MC, V.

$$ WHITE SWAN INN. A library with book-lined walls and a crackling fire is the heartbeat of the White Swan, and wine, cheese, and afternoon tea are served in the lounge, where comfortable chairs and sofas encourage lingering. Each of the good-size rooms in this wonderfully warm and inviting inn has a gas fireplace, private bath, refrigerator, and reproduction Edwardian furniture. The breakfasts (included in the room rate) are famous, and you can buy the inn's cookbook and take a crack at crab-and-cheese soufflé toasts, chocolate scones, or artichoke pesto puffs at home. 845 Bush St., 94108, tel. 415/775–1755 or 800/999–9570, fax 415/775–5717, www.foursisters.com. 23 rooms, 3 suites. Breakfast room, in-room data ports, no-smoking floor, refrigerators, gym, dry cleaning, laundry service, concierge, meeting room, parking (fee). AE, MC, V.

$–$$ BIJOU. With plush velvet upholstery and rich detailing, this hotel is a nostalgic tribute to 1930s cinema. The lobby's tiny theater, Le Petit Theatre Bijou, treats guests to screenings from the hotel's collection of 65 San Francisco–theme films—from *The Maltese Falcon* to *What's Up Doc?* The smallish but cheerful rooms are decorated with black-and-white movie stills. For those who want to be in pictures, the handcrafted chrome ticket booth in the lobby has a hot line with information on current San Francisco film shoots seeking extras. *111 Mason St., at Eddy St., 94102, tel. 415/771–1200 or 800/771–1022, fax 415/346–3196, www.hotelbijou.com. 65 rooms. No-smoking room, laundry service, concierge, parking (fee). AE, D, DC, MC, V.*

$–$$ GOLDEN GATE HOTEL. Captain Nemo, a 25-pound black-and-white cat who must live very well indeed, serves as the unofficial doorman for this homey, family-run B&B three blocks northwest of Union Square. Built in 1913 as a hotel, the four-story Edwardian has a yellow-and-cream facade with black trim, and bay windows front and back. The original "birdcage" elevator lifts you to hallways lined with historical photographs and guest rooms individually decorated with antiques, wicker pieces, and Laura Ashley bedding and curtains. *775 Bush St., 94108, tel. 415/392–3702 or 800/835–1118, fax 415/392–6202, www.goldengatehotel.com. 25 rooms, 14 with bath. No-smoking floor, parking (fee). AE, DC, MC, V.*

$ ADELAIDE INN. The bedspreads at this quiet retreat may not match the drapes or carpets, and the floors may creak, but the rooms are sunny, clean, and remarkably cheap. Tucked away in an alley, the funky European-style pension hosts many guests from Germany, France, and Italy, making it fun to chat over complimentary coffee and rolls downstairs in the mornings. There are sinks in every room, but all baths (down the hall) are shared. *5 Isadora Duncan Ct., at Taylor St. between Geary and Post Sts., 94102, tel. 415/441–2474 or 415/441–2261, fax 415/441–0161. 18 rooms with shared bath. Breakfast room, in-room data ports. AE, MC, V.*

$ GRANT PLAZA HOTEL. One block in from the Chinatown Gate
★ guarded by its famous stone lions, this hotel may seem worlds away from Union Square, yet it and the Financial District are only

a stone's throw away. Amazingly low room rates for this part of town make the Grant Plaza a find for budget travelers wanting to look out their window at the striking architecture and fascinating street life of Chinatown. The smallish rooms, all with private baths, are very clean and modern. Rooms on the top floor are newer, slightly brighter, and a bit more expensive; for a quieter stay ask for one in the back. All rooms have electronic locks, voice mail, and satellite TV. *465 Grant Ave., 94108, tel. 415/434–3883 or 800/472–6899, fax 415/434–3886, www.grantplaza.com. 71 rooms, 1 suite. Concierge, business services, parking (fee). AE, DC, MC, V.*

FINANCIAL DISTRICT

$$$$ **HYATT REGENCY.** The gray concrete exterior of this hotel, at the
★ foot of Market Street and next to the Embarcadero Center, is an unlikely introduction to the world's largest atrium lobby—a spectacular 17-story display with full-size trees, a running stream, and huge fountain. Rooms, some with bay-view balconies and all with city or bay views, have a handsome, contemporary look with blond-wood furniture and ergonomic desk chairs. The Equinox, San Francisco's only revolving rooftop restaurant, rotates atop the hotel like a crown jewel. *5 Embarcadero Center, 94111, tel. 415/788–1234 or 800/233–1234, fax 415/398–2567, www.hyatt.com. 760 rooms, 45 suites. 2 restaurants, bar, lobby lounge, in-room data ports, in-room safes, no-smoking floor, room service, gym, concierge, business services, meeting rooms, parking (fee). AE, D, DC, MC, V.*

$$$$ **MANDARIN ORIENTAL.** Since the Mandarin comprises the top
★ 11 floors (38 to 48) of San Francisco's third-tallest building, all rooms provide sweeping panoramic vistas of the city and beyond. The glass-enclosed sky bridges that connect the east and west towers of the hotel are almost as striking as the views. Rooms facing west fill up quickly because of their dramatic views of the Golden Gate Bridge and the Pacific Ocean. And because the windows actually open, unlike in many modern buildings, you can hear the "ding ding" of the California Street cable cars down below

as you peer miles into the scenic distance (the hotel provides binoculars). The Mandarin Rooms in each tower have extra deep bathtubs right next to picture windows; enjoy a decadent bathing experience above the city with loofah sponges, plush robes, and silk slippers. *222 Sansome St., 94104, tel. 415/276–9888 or 800/622–0404, fax 415/433–0289, www.mandarinoriental.com. 154 rooms, 4 suites. Lobby lounge, in-room data ports, in-room safes, minibars, no-smoking floor, room service, gym, dry cleaning, laundry service, concierge, business services, meeting room, parking (fee). AE, D, DC, MC, V.*

$$$$ PALACE HOTEL. This landmark hotel—with a guest list that has included Thomas Edison, Amelia Earhart, Bing Crosby, and 10 American presidents—was the world's largest and most luxurious hotel when it opened in 1875. Completely rebuilt after the earthquake and fire of 1906 (which sent Italian opera star Enrico Caruso into the street wearing nothing but a towel and vowing never to return to San Francisco), today the splendid hotel includes a stunning entryway and the fabulous Belle Epoque Garden Court restaurant, with its graceful chandeliers and stained-glass dome ceiling. Rooms, with twice-daily maid service and nightly turndown, have high ceilings, antique reproduction furnishings, and marble bathrooms with luxury bath products. The hotel's 20-yard indoor lap pool is the longest hotel pool in the city. *2 New Montgomery St., 94105, tel. 415/512–1111, fax 415/543–0671. 518 rooms, 34 suites. 3 restaurants, bar, room service, indoor lap pool, health club, laundry service, parking (fee). AE, D, DC, MC, V.*

$$$$ PARK HYATT. Contemporary in design but with a touch of old-world style, the Park Hyatt is a well-managed property across Battery Street from the Embarcadero Center, six blocks west of the waterfront. The hotel's public areas have large floral displays and fine artworks on the walls. The good-size rooms have Australian lacewood, polished granite, stylish contemporary furniture, and fresh flowers. Amenities include voice mail and Neutrogena toiletries. Complimentary car service is offered within downtown San Francisco. *333 Battery St., 94111, tel. 415/392–1234* or 800/492–8822, fax 415/421–2433, www.hyatt.com. 323 rooms, 37 suites. Restaurant, 2 bars, in-room data ports, minibars, room service, gym, dry cleaning, laundry service, business services, parking (fee). AE, D, DC, MC, V.

$$$ ★ **HARBOR COURT.** Within shouting distance of the Bay Bridge and the hot South of Market area with its plentiful nightclubs and restaurants, this cozy hotel, formerly an Army/Navy YMCA, is noted for the exemplary service of its warm, friendly staff. Some guest rooms, with double sets of soundproof windows, overlook the bay; others face a dressed-up rooftop. Rooms are smallish but have fancy touches such as partially canopied, plushly upholstered beds; tastefully faux-textured walls, and fine reproductions of late-19th-century nautical and nature prints. In the evening complimentary wine is served in the cozy lounge, sometimes accompanied by live guitar. 165 Steuart St., 94105, tel. 415/882–1300 or 800/346–0555, fax 415/882–1313, www.harborcourt. com. 130 rooms, 1 suite. In-room data ports, minibars, no-smoking floor, room service, dry cleaning, laundry service, business services, parking (fee). AE, D, DC, MC, V.

SOUTH OF MARKET (SOMA)

$$$$ **THE ARGENT.** This hotel rises 36 stories over the bustling downtown and South of Market areas and is within a block or two of several major museums. It has a luxuriously appointed lobby and a handsome, clublike lounge with live music every evening but Sunday. Bright and airy guest rooms have floor-to-ceiling picture windows. About half of the larger-than-average rooms face south and are especially sunny, overlooking Yerba Buena Gardens and the city, bay, and hills beyond. The equally scenic rooms on the north side peer through the tall buildings of the Financial District, occasionally affording a glimpse of the Golden Gate Bridge, the bay, and Alcatraz. 50 3rd St., 94103, tel. 415/974–6400 or 877/222–6699, fax 415/543–8268, www.argenthotel.com. 641 rooms, 26 suites. Restaurant, bar, lobby lounge, in-room data ports, in-

room safes, no-smoking floor, refrigerators, room service, massage, health club, dry cleaning, laundry service, concierge, business services, convention center, meeting rooms, parking (fee). AE, D, DC, MC, V.

$$$$ HOTEL PALOMAR. ★ Famous "boutique hotel" trailblazer Bill Kimpton (Hotel Monaco) transformed the top five floors of the green-tiled and turreted 1908 Pacific Place Building into an urbane and luxurious oasis above the busiest part of the city. You enter the hotel under a glass-and-steel fan-shape canopy into a spare, modern lobby with a harlequin-pattern wooden floor and stylish gunmetal and brass registration desk. Rooms have muted leopard-pattern carpeting, walls covered in raffia weave, and bold navy-and-cream stripe drapes. The look is reminiscent of the 1940s, but the cordless phones, CD players, and all-in-one faxing-copying-printing machines are definitely modern. Aveda products are found in the sparkling baths, where a "tub menu" including various herbal and botanical infusions awaits you. *12 Fourth St., 94103, tel. 415/348–1111 or 877/294–9711, fax 415/348–0302, www.hotelpalomar.com. 182 rooms, 16 suites. Restaurant, bar, lobby lounge, in-room data ports, minibars, no-smoking floor, room service, gym, dry cleaning, laundry service, concierge, business services, meeting room, parking (fee). AE, D, DC, MC, V.*

$$$$ SAN FRANCISCO MARRIOTT. When this huge 40-story hotel opened in 1989, critics alternately raved about and condemned its distinctive design—modern art deco, with large fanlike windows across the top (it's called the "jukebox Marriott" by locals). The glitzy lobby has a mirror ceiling and a 40-ft beaded crystal chandelier. An adjacent five-story glass-topped atrium encloses the dining court (two restaurants and a lounge) lush with tropical plants. An impressive collection of original paintings and sculptures graces the public areas. The functional though bland standard rooms have chain-type decor, but some have excellent views. Some of the more interesting suites are split-level with spiral staircases. Conventioneers often stay here, and it's a good choice for art buffs hoping to visit the nearby San Francisco

Museum of Modern Art and the Yerba Buena Center. 55 4th St., 94103, tel. 415/896–1600 or 800/228–9290, fax 415/896–6177. 1,366 rooms, 134 suites. 3 restaurants, bar, 2 piano bars, sports bar, in-room data ports, minibars, room service, pool, hot tub, sauna, gym, dry cleaning, laundry service, concierge, business services, convention center, meeting room, car rental, parking (fee). AE, D, DC, MC, V.

$$$$ W SAN FRANCISCO. Epitomizing cool modernity and urban chic both in its decor and in the crowd it attracts, the 31-story W San Francisco has become the place to drink, dine, and stay in the new center of San Francisco. Contributing to its success, of course, has been its prime location next to SFMOMA. The severity of stone, corrugated metal, frosted glass, and other industrial elements in the public spaces is offset by accents of polished mahogany and broad-stripe carpeting. Dimly lit hallways lead to smallish guest rooms, each with either a cozy corner sitting area or an upholstered window seat. The luxurious beds have pillow-top mattresses and goose-down comforters and pillows. Cordless phones, Aveda bath products, and stereos with CD players are added bonuses. 181 3rd St., 94103, tel. 415/777–5300 or 877/946–8357, fax 415/817–7823, www.whotels.com. 418 rooms, 5 suites. Restaurant, bar, café, in-room data ports, in-room safes, minibars, no-smoking floor, in-room VCRs, refrigerators, room service, pool, hot tub, massage, gym, dry cleaning, laundry service, concierge, business services, meeting room, parking (fee). AE, D, DC, MC, V.

$$–$$$ HOTEL MILANO. Adjacent to the San Francisco Shopping Centre and Nordstrom and a stone's throw from all the museums and attractions south of Market Street, this hotel is a shopper's and culture maven's delight. The eight-story hotel's stately 1913 neoclassic facade gives way to a warm and stylish lobby with a large Alexander Calder–style mobile over the lounge area. Guest rooms are spacious and handsomely decorated in warm earth tones with contemporary Italian furnishings. Weary shoppers and museum goers can soak, steam, or bake away fatigue in the split-level fitness center on the seventh and eighth floors. 55 5th

St., 94103, tel. 415/543–8555 or 800/398–7555, fax 415/543–5885, hotelmilano.citysearch.com. 108 rooms. Restaurant, bar, sushi bar, in-room data ports, in-room safes, minibars, no-smoking floor, room service, hot tub, sauna, steam room, gym, dry cleaning, laundry service, concierge, business services, meeting room, parking (fee). AE, D, DC, MC, V.

NOB HILL

$$$$ ★ **THE FAIRMONT.** Commanding the top of Nob Hill like a European palace, the Fairmont, which served as the model for the St. Gregory in the TV series Hotel, has experienced plenty of real-life drama: It served as city headquarters during the 1906 earthquake and hosted dignitaries who penned the charter for the United Nations in 1945 (the 40 flags out front represent the nations signing the charter). In 1999–2000, the hotel restored architect Julia Morgan's original, elegant 1907 interiors. Guest rooms, in either buttery yellow, pale cantaloupe, or light-blue color schemes, all have high ceilings, fine dark-wood furniture, and colorful Asian touches such as Chinese porcelain lamps. Don't forget happy hour at the Tonga Room, complete with tiki huts, a live band floating in a tropical lagoon, and a thunderstorm every half hour. 950 Mason St., 94108, tel. 415/772–5000 or 800/527–4727, fax 415/ 837–0587, www.fairmont.com. 531 rooms, 65 suites. 3 restaurants, 4 bars, in-room data ports, minibars, no-smoking room, room service, barbershop, hair salon, health club, nightclub, baby-sitting, dry cleaning, laundry service, concierge, business services, meeting room, car rental, parking (fee). AE, D, DC, MC, V.

$$$$ **MARK HOPKINS INTER-CONTINENTAL.** A circular drive leads up to this regal Nob Hill landmark with elaborate Spanish Renaissance terra-cotta ornaments atop the central tower and two stately wings. The lobby has copper-color upholstered walls, overstuffed chairs on handwoven carpets, and its original 1926 marble floor intact. Rooms have custom-made maple furniture stained in cherry or walnut. Baths have black granite vanity tops and Spanish and Italian marble walls and floors. Rooms on the upper floors have views of either the Golden Gate Bridge or the downtown cityscape. Prince Phillip, Liz Taylor, and Elvis Presley have all boogied here. *999 California St., 94108, tel. 415/392–3434 or 800/ 662–4455, fax 415/421–3302, www.markhopkins.net. 342 rooms, 38 suites. Restaurant, 2 bars, room service, gym, dry cleaning, laundry service, concierge, business services, meeting room, car rental, parking (fee). AE, D, DC, MC, V.*

$$$$ ★ **RITZ-CARLTON, SAN FRANCISCO.** This world-class hotel is a stunning tribute to beauty; splendor; and warm, sincere service. Beyond the neoclassic facade with its 17 Ionic columns (the building was originally Met Life's headquarters in 1909), crystal chandeliers illuminate an opulent lobby adorned with Georgian antiques and a collection of museum-quality 18th- and 19th-century paintings. The hotel's fitness center is a destination in its own right, with an indoor swimming pool, steam baths, saunas, and a whirlpool. The luxuriously appointed rooms have feather beds with 300-count Egyptian cotton sheets and down comforters. Afternoon tea in the Lobby Lounge—which overlooks the hotel's beautifully landscaped garden courtyard—is a San Francisco institution. *600 Stockton St., at California St., 94108, tel. 415/296–7465 or 800/241–3333, fax 415/986–1268, www.ritzcarlton.com. 294 rooms, 42 suites. 2 restaurants, 3 bars, lobby lounge, in-room data ports, indoor pool, hot tub, sauna, health club, dry cleaning, laundry service, concierge, concierge floor, business services, meeting room, parking (fee). AE, D, DC, MC, V.*

$$$–$$$$ **THE HUNTINGTON HOTEL.** The family-owned, ivy-covered redbrick Huntington Hotel provides an oasis of gracious personal service in an atmosphere of understated luxury. The privacy of the hotel's many celebrated guests, from Bogart and Bacall to Picasso and Pavarotti, has always been impeccably preserved. Rooms and suites, many of which have great views of Grace Cathedral, the bay, or the city skyline, are large because they used to be residential apartments. Most rooms have wet bars, all have large antique desks, and some suites have kitchens. *1075 California St., 94108,* tel. 415/474–5400 or 800/227–4683, fax 415/474–6227, www. huntingtonhotel.com. 100 rooms, 35 suites. Restaurant, bar, in-room data ports, in-room safes, no-smoking rooms, room service, indoor pool, massage, sauna, spa, steam room, dry cleaning, laundry service, concierge, meeting room, parking (fee). AE, D, DC, MC, V.

$$$–$$$$ **NOB HILL LAMBOURNE.** This urban retreat, designed with the traveling executive in mind, takes pride in pampering business travelers with personal computers, fax machines, personalized voice mail, and a small on-site spa with massages, body scrubs, manicures, and pedicures. If that's not enough, videos on such topics as stress reduction and yoga are available on request, rooms come with white-noise machines and rice-hull pillows, and vitamins and chamomile tea arrive with turndown service. Rooms have queen-size beds with hand-sewn mattresses, silk-damask bedding, and contemporary furnishings in muted colors. 725 Pine St., at Stockton St., 94108, tel. 415/433–2287 or 800/274–8466, fax 415/433–0975, www.nobhilllambourne.com. 14 rooms, 6 suites. In-room data ports, no-smoking floor, in-room VCRs, massage, spa, business services, parking (fee). AE, D, DC, MC, V.

FISHERMAN'S WHARF/NORTH BEACH

$$$–$$$$ **MARRIOTT AT FISHERMAN'S WHARF.** Behind an unremarkable sand-color facade, the Marriott strikes a grand note with its lavish, low-ceiling lobby with marble floors, a double fireplace, and English club–style furniture. Rooms, all with forest-green, burgundy, and cream color schemes, were renovated in 1998 and have either a king-size bed or two double beds. Restaurant Spada 2 serves breakfast, lunch, and dinner, while lunch is also served in the lobby lounge. 1250 Columbus Ave., 94133, tel. 415/775–7555 or 800/228–9290, fax 415/474–2099, www.marriott.com. 269 rooms, 16 suites. Restaurant, bar, lobby lounge, in-room data ports, minibars, no-smoking floor, sauna, health club, piano, dry cleaning, laundry service, concierge, business services, meeting rooms, parking (fee). AE, D, DC, MC, V.

\$\$–\$\$\$ **RADISSON HOTEL AT FISHERMAN'S WHARF.** Occupying an
★ entire city block, and part of a complex including 25 shops and restaurants, this is the only bayfront hotel at Fisherman's Wharf and the nearest to Pier 39 and the bay cruise docks. The medium-size lobby has plenty of comfortable couches and chairs. Eighty percent of the rooms have views of the bay and overlook a landscaped courtyard and pool. Rooms are simple and bright. *250 Beach St., 94133, tel. 415/392–6700 or 800/333–3333, fax 415/986–7853, www.radisson.com. 355 rooms. 3 restaurants, in-room data ports, no-smoking room, pool, gym, concierge, parking (fee). AE, D, DC, MC, V.*

\$\$ **HOTEL BOHÈME.** The Bohème, in the middle of historic North Beach, takes you back in time with coral-color walls, bistro tables, and memorabilia recalling the Beat generation. Allen Ginsberg, who stayed here many times, could in his later years be seen sitting in a window tapping away on his laptop computer. Screenwriters from Francis Ford Coppola's nearby American Zoetrope studio stay here often, as do poets and other artists. Beds have unnecessary but fun mosquito netting and baths have cheerful yellow tiles. Rooms in the rear are quieter. Complimentary sherry is served in the lobby. *444 Columbus Ave., 94133, tel. 415/433–9111, fax 415/362–6292, www.hotelboheme.com. 16 rooms. In-room data ports, no-smoking floor. AE, D, DC, MC, V.*

\$ **SAN REMO.** This three-story, blue-and-white 1906 Italianate
★ Victorian just a few blocks from Fisherman's Wharf (in an older, more authentic section of North Beach) was once home to longshoremen and Beats. A narrow stairway from the street leads to the front desk, and labyrinthine hallways route you to the small but charming rooms with lace curtains, forest-green wooden floors, brass beds, and other antique furnishings. All rooms eschew phones and TVs. The upper floors are brighter, being closer to the skylights that provide sunshine to the many potted plants in the brass-banistered hallways. About a third of the rooms have sinks; all rooms share scrupulously clean black-and-

white tile shower and toilet facilities with pull-chain toilets. 2237 Mason St., 94133, tel. 415/776–8688 or 800/352–7366, fax 415/776–2811, www.sanremohotel.com. 62 rooms. Coin laundry, parking (fee). AE, DC, MC, V.

PACIFIC HEIGHTS, COW HOLLOW, AND THE MARINA

$$$$ SHERMAN HOUSE. ★ This magnificent Italianate mansion at the foot of residential Pacific Heights is San Francisco's most luxurious small hotel. Rooms are individually decorated with Biedermeier, English Jacobean, or French Second Empire antiques. The decadent mood is enhanced by tapestrylike canopies over four-poster feather beds; wood-burning fireplaces with marble mantels; and sumptuous bathrooms, all with whirlpool baths. The six romantic suites attract honeymooners from around the world. Room rates include evening wine and hors d'oeuvres in an upstairs sitting room. 2160 Green St., 94123, tel. 415/563–3600 or 800/424–5777, fax 415/563–1882, www.theshermanhouse.com. 8 rooms, 6 suites. Dining room, room service, in-room VCRs, piano, concierge, free parking. AE, D, DC, MC, V.

$$$ EL DRISCO HOTEL. In one of the wealthiest and most beautiful residential neighborhoods in San Francisco, the understatedly elegant El Drisco is a quiet haven for anyone overwhelmed by the busier parts of the city. Understandably, the hotel serves as a celebrity hideaway from time to time; Val Kilmer and Linda Ronstadt are former guests. Some of the 1903 Edwardian rooms, pale yellow and white and outfitted with genteel furnishings and luxury amenities (you can take the plush little slippers home), face the Golden Gate Bridge; others have a commanding view of the eastern or southern parts of the city. Each night at turndown, the staff leaves an oatmeal cookie and the next day's weather forecast. Continental breakfast (included in the room rate) is served in the sunny breakfast room on a lower floor, and there is a lovely sitting room off the lobby. 2901 Pacific Ave., 94115, tel. 415/346–2880 or

800/634–7277, fax 415/567–5537, www.eldriscohotel.com. 33 rooms, 15 suites. Breakfast room, in-room data ports, minibars, no-smoking room, refrigerators, in-room VCRs, gym, dry cleaning, laundry service, concierge. AE, D, DC, MC, V.

$$–$$$ **UNION STREET INN.** Innkeeper David Coyle was a chef for the
★ Duke and Duchess of Bedford, England, and his partner Jane Bertorelli has been innkeeping since 1984. With the help of Jane's many family heirlooms, they've made this 1902 Edwardian a delightful B&B inn filled with antiques and unique artwork. Equipped with candles, fresh flowers, and wineglasses, rooms are very popular with honeymooners. The private Carriage House, which has its own whirlpool tub and shower under a skylight, is separated from the main house by an old-fashioned English garden complete with lemon trees. An elaborate complimentary breakfast is served in the parlor, in the garden, or in your rooms. 2229 Union St., 94123, tel. 415/346–0424, fax 415/922–8046, www.unionstreetinn.com. 6 rooms. Breakfast room, no-smoking room, parking (fee). AE, MC, V.

$$ **BED AND BREAKFAST INN.** Hidden in a mew off Union Street between Buchanan and Laguna, this ivy-covered Victorian (San Francisco's first B&B) contains English country–style rooms full of antiques, plants, and floral paintings. Though the rooms with shared baths are quite small, the other rooms and two suites have ample space. The Mayfair, a bi-level apartment above the main house, has a living room, kitchenette, and a sleeping loft. 4 Charlton Ct., at Union St. 94123, tel. 415/921–9784, fax 415/921–0544, www.thebandb.com. 8 rooms, 3 with shared bath; 2 suites. Breakfast room, kitchenettes (some), parking (fee). MC, V.

$$ **HOTEL DEL SOL.** Once a typical 1950s-style motor court, the
★ Hotel Del Sol is an anything-but-typical artistic statement playfully celebrating California's vibrant (some might say wacky) culture. The sunny courtyard and yellow-and-blue three-story building are candy for the eyes. Rooms face boldly striped patios, citrus trees,

and a hammock and heated swimming pool under towering palm trees. Even the carports have striped dividing drapes. Rooms have plantation shutters, tropical-stripe bedspreads, and rattan chairs. Some rooms have brick fireplaces, and suites for families with small children include bunk beds, child-friendly furnishings, a kitchenette, and games. There are even free kites for kids. *3100 Webster St., 94123, tel. 415/921–5520 or 877/433–5765, fax 415/931–4137, www.thehoteldelsol.com. 47 rooms, 10 suites. In-room data ports, in-room safes, kitchenettes (some), no-smoking room, pool, sauna, laundry service, concierge, free parking. AE, D, DC, MC, V.*

$ COW HOLLOW MOTOR INN AND SUITES. Built by the same family that runs it, this large, modern hotel has interior corridors and rooms that are more spacious than average, with sitting-dining areas and dark-wood furniture. Some rooms have views of the Golden Gate Bridge. The large suites ($195–$245) seem like typical San Francisco apartments with their hardwood floors, Oriental carpets, antique furnishings, marble fireplaces, and fully equipped kitchens. *2190 Lombard St., 94123, tel. 415/921–5800, fax 415/922–8515. 117 rooms, 12 suites. Restaurant, kitchenettes (some), no-smoking floor, meeting room, free parking. AE, DC, MC, V.*

$ PACIFIC HEIGHTS INN. One of the most genteel-looking motels in town, this two-story motor court near the busy intersection of Union Street and Van Ness is dressed up with wrought-iron railings and benches, hanging plants, and pebble exterior walkways facing onto the parking lot. Rooms are on the small side. Most of the units are suites, some with full kitchens, some with extra bedrooms. Morning pastries and coffee are served in the lobby. *1555 Union St., 94123, tel. 415/776–3310 or 800/523–1801, fax 415/776–8176, www.pacificheightsinn.com. 15 rooms, 25 suites. Kitchenettes (some), no-smoking room, free parking. AE, D, DC, MC, V.*

CIVIC CENTER/VAN NESS

$$$ THE ARCHBISHOP'S MANSION. Everything here is extravagantly ★ romantic, starting with the cavernous common areas, where a chandelier used in the movie *Gone With the Wind* hangs above a 1904 Bechstein grand piano once owned by Noel Coward. The 15 guest rooms, each named for a famous opera, are individually decorated with intricately carved antiques; many have whirlpool tubs or fireplaces (there are 16 fireplaces in the mansion). Though not within easy walking distance of many restaurants or attractions, its perch on the corner of Alamo Square near the Painted Ladies— San Francisco's famous Victorian homes—makes for a scenic, relaxed stay. *1000 Fulton St., 94117, tel. 415/563–7872 or 800/543– 5820, fax 415/885–3193, www.archbishopsmansion.com. 10 rooms, 5 suites. Breakfast room, in-room data ports, no-smoking room, in-room VCRs, piano, meeting room, free parking. AE, MC, V.*

$$$ HOTEL MAJESTIC. One of San Francisco's original grand hotels, this five-story white 1902 Edwardian was once the decade-long residence of screen stars Joan Fontaine and Olivia de Havilland. Complimentary wine and hors d'oeuvres are served afternoons in the exquisite lobby, replete with glistening granite stairs, antique chandeliers, plush Victorian chairs, and a white-marble fireplace. The hotel's Perlot restaurant has an American prix-fixe menu, as well as 24-hour room service. Glass cases in the bar house a stunning collection of rare butterflies from Africa and New Guinea. Guest rooms and baths are presently being transformed from their antiques-laden look to something lighter and more contemporary. For a $10 fee you'll have access to a nearby fitness center with a pool and tennis courts. *1500 Sutter St., 94109, tel. 415/ 441–1100 or 800/869–8869, fax 415/673–7331, www. thehotelmajestic.com. 49 rooms, 9 suites. Restaurant, bar, room service, dry cleaning, laundry service, parking (fee). AE, DC, MC, V.*

$$$ RADISSON MIYAKO HOTEL. Adjacent to the Japantown complex and three blocks from Fillmore Street and Pacific Heights, this pagoda-style hotel is popular with business travelers. Some guest rooms are in the tower building; others are in the garden wing, which has a traditional Japanese garden with a waterfall. Japanese-style rooms have futon beds with tatami mats, while Western rooms have traditional beds with mattresses; all have gorgeous Asian furniture and original artwork. Most have their own soaking rooms with a bucket and stool and a Japanese tub (1 ft deeper than Western tubs), and in-room shiatsu massages are available. *1625 Post St., at Laguna St., 94115, tel. 415/922–3200 or 800/533–4567, fax 415/921–0417, www.miyakohotel.com. 211 rooms, 17 suites. Restaurant, bar, in-room data ports, minibars, massage, gym, dry cleaning, laundry service, business services. AE, D, DC, MC, V.*

$$–$$$ **INN AT THE OPERA.** This seven-story hotel a block or so from city
★ hall, Davies Symphony Hall, and the War Memorial Opera House has hosted the likes of Pavarotti and Baryshnikov, as well as lesser lights of the music, dance, and opera worlds. Behind the marble-floor lobby are rooms of various sizes with creamy pastels and dark-wood furnishings. The bureau drawers are lined with sheet music, and every room includes a queen-size bed, terry robes, and a microwave oven. A major attraction is the sumptuous, dimly lighted Ovation restaurant. Stars congregate in its mahogany and green-velvet interior before and after performances. *333 Fulton St., 94102, tel. 415/863–8400 or 800/325–2708, fax 415/861–0821. 30 rooms, 18 suites. Restaurant, lobby lounge, room service, concierge, parking (fee). AE, DC, MC, V.*

$$ **PHOENIX HOTEL.** From the piped-in, poolside jungle music to the aquatic-theme, ultrahip Backflip restaurant and lounge immersed in shimmering hues of blue and green, the Phoenix evokes the tropics—or at least a fun, kitschy version of it. Although probably not the place for a traveling executive seeking peace and quiet—or anyone put off by its location on the fringes of the seedy Tenderloin District—the Phoenix does boast a list of celebrity guests, including such big-name bands as R.E.M. and Pearl Jam. Rooms are simple, with handmade bamboo furniture, tropical-print bedspreads, and original art by local artists. All rooms face the courtyard pool (with a mural by Francis Forlenza on its bottom) and sculpture garden. Continental breakfast is included in the room rate. *601 Eddy St., 94109, tel. 415/776–1380 or 800/248–*

9466, fax 415/885–3109, www.jdvhospitality.com. 41 rooms, 3 suites. Restaurant, bar, room service, pool, massage, nightclub, laundry service, free parking. AE, D, DC, MC, V.

THE AIRPORT

$$$$ ★ **HOTEL SOFITEL–SAN FRANCISCO BAY.** Parisian boulevard lampposts, a métro sign, and a kiosk covered with posters bring an unexpected bit of Paris to this bay-side hotel. The French-theme public spaces—the Gigi Brasserie, Baccarat Restaurant, and La Terrasse bar—have a light, open, airy feeling that extends to the rooms, each of which has a minibar and writing desk. *223 Twin Dolphin Dr., Redwood City 94065, tel. 650/598–9000 or 800/763–4835, fax 650/598–0459, www.sofitel.com. 379 rooms, 42 suites. 2 restaurants, bar, lobby lounge, minibars, health club, laundry service, concierge, meeting room, free parking. AE, DC, MC, V.*

$$–$$$$ ★ **EMBASSY SUITES SAN FRANCISCO AIRPORT–BURLINGAME.** With excellent service and facilities, this California Mission–style hostelry is one of the most lavish in the airport area. Set on the bay with up-close views of planes taking off and landing, it consists entirely of suites that open onto a nine-story atrium and tropical garden replete with ducks, parrots, fish, and a waterfall. Living rooms all have a work area, sleeper sofa, wet bar, television, microwave, and refrigerator. Rates include a full breakfast. *150 Anza Blvd., Burlingame 94010, tel. 650/342–4600 or 800/362–2779, fax 650/343–8137, www.embassyburlingame.com. 340 suites. Restaurant, bar, no-smoking rooms, refrigerators, room service, pool, sauna, gym, concierge, business services, free parking. AE, DC, MC, V.*

$$–$$$$ ★ **HYATT REGENCY SAN FRANCISCO AIRPORT.** A spectacular 10-story lobby atrium encompasses 29,000 square ft of this dramatic hotel 2 mi south of the airport. This is the largest airport convention hotel in northern California, providing a high level of personal service for business and leisure travelers alike. Almost every service and amenity you could think of is here, including athletic facilities and several dining and entertainment options. Rooms

Hotel How-Tos

Where you stay does make a difference. Do you prefer a modern high-rise or an intimate B&B? A center-city location or the quiet suburbs? What facilities do you want? Sort through your priorities, then price it all out.

HOW TO GET A DEAL After you've chosen a likely candidate or two, phone them directly and price a room for your travel dates. Then call the hotel's toll-free number and ask the same questions. Also try consolidators and hotel-room discounters. You won't hear the same rates twice. On the spot, make a reservation as soon as you are quoted a price you want to pay.

PROMISES, PROMISES If you have special requests, make them when you reserve. Get written confirmation of any promises.

SETTLE IN Upon arriving, make sure everything works—lights and lamps, TV and radio, sink, tub, shower, and anything else that matters. Report any problems immediately. And don't wait until you need extra pillows or blankets or an ironing board to call housekeeping. Also check out the fire emergency instructions. Know where to find the fire exits, and make sure your companions do, too.

IF YOU NEED TO COMPLAIN Be polite but firm. Explain the problem to the person in charge. Suggest a course of action. If you aren't satisfied, repeat your requests to the manager. Document everything: Take pictures and keep a written record of who you've spoken with, when, and what was said. Contact your travel agent, if he made the reservations.

KNOW THE SCORE When you go out, take your hotel's business cards (one for everyone in your party). If you have extras, you can give them out to new acquaintances who want to call you.

TIP UP FRONT For special services, a tip or partial tip in advance can work wonders.

USE ALL THE HOTEL RESOURCES A concierge can make difficult things easy. But a desk clerk, bellhop, or other hotel employee who's friendly, smart, and ambitious can often steer you straight as well. A gratuity is in order if the advice is helpful.

are modern and well equipped. Scalini serves upscale northern Italian fare. *1333 Bayshore Hwy., Burlingame 94010, tel. 650/347–1234, fax 650/696–2669, www.sanfrancisco.hyatt.com. 767 rooms, 26 suites. Restaurant, café, deli, lobby lounge, piano bar, sports bar, in-room data ports, no-smoking floor, room service, pool, outdoor hot tub, gym, jogging, dry cleaning, laundry service, concierge, business services, convention center, meeting room, airport shuttle, car rental, parking (fee). AE, D, DC, MC, V.*

PRACTICAL INFORMATION

Air Travel to and from San Francisco

Heavy fog is infamous for causing chronic delays in and out of San Francisco. Travelers heading to the East and South Bay should make every effort to fly into either the Oakland or San Jose airports. The Oakland airport, which is easy to navigate and is accessible by public transit, is a good alternative to San Francisco's airport.

CARRIERS

➤ **MAJOR AIRLINES: American** (tel. 800/433–7300). **British Airways** (tel. 800/247–9297). **Cathay Pacific** (tel. 800/233–2742). **Continental** (tel. 800/231–0856). **Delta** (tel. 800/221–1212). **Japan Air Lines** (tel. 800/525–3663). **Northwest/KLM** (tel. 800/225–2525). **United** (tel. 800/241–6522). **US Airways** (tel. 800/428–4322).

➤ **FROM THE U.K.: American** (tel. 0345/789–789). **British Airways** (tel. 0345/222–111). **Delta** (tel. 0800/414–767). **United** (tel. 0800/888–555). **Virgin Atlantic** (tel. 01293/747–747).

Airports & Transfers

➤ **AIRPORT INFORMATION: San Francisco International Airport (SFO)** (tel. 650/761–0800). **Oakland International Airport** (tel. 510/577–4000). **San Jose International Airport** (tel. 408/277–4759).

TRANSFERS FROM SAN FRANCISCO INTERNATIONAL AIRPORT

A taxi ride from SFO to downtown costs about $30. Airport shuttles are inexpensive and efficient. The SFO Airporter ($10) picks up passengers at baggage claim (lower level) and serves selected downtown hotels. SuperShuttle stops at the upper-level traffic islands and takes you from the airport to anywhere within the city limits of San Francisco. It costs from $10 to $12 depending on your destination. Inexpensive shuttles to the East Bay (among them Bayporter Express) also depart from SFO's upper-level traffic islands; expect to pay around $20. The cheapest way to get from the airport to San Francisco is via SamTrans Bus 292 (55 minutes; $2.20) and KX (35 minutes; $3; only one small carry-on bag permitted) to San Francisco or Bus BX to the Colma BART train station. Board the SamTrans buses at the north end of the lower level.

To drive to downtown San Francisco from the airport, take U.S. 101 north to the Civic Center (9th Street), 7th Street, or 4th Street exit. If you're headed to the Embarcadero or Fisherman's Wharf, take I–280 north (the exit is to the right, just past 3Com Park) and get off at the 4th Street/King Street exit. King Street becomes the Embarcadero a few blocks east of the exit. The Embarcadero winds around the waterfront to Fisherman's Wharf.

TRANSFERS FROM OAKLAND INTERNATIONAL AIRPORT

A taxi from Oakland's airport to downtown San Francisco costs between $30 and $35. America's Shuttle, Bayporter Express, and other shuttles serve major hotels and provide door-to-door service to the East Bay and San Francisco. Marin Door to Door serves Marin County for a flat $50 fee. The best way to get to San Francisco via public transit is to take the AIR BART bus ($2) to the Coliseum/Oakland International Airport BART station (BART fares vary depending on where you're going; the ride to downtown San Francisco costs $2.75).

If you're driving from Oakland International Airport, take Hegenberger Road east to I–880 north to I–80 west.

TRANSFERS FROM SAN JOSE INTERNATIONAL AIRPORT

A taxi from the airport to downtown San Jose costs about $12 (a taxi to San Francisco costs about $100). South & East Bay Airport

Shuttle transports you to the South Bay and East Bay. A shuttle to downtown San Jose costs $15. VIP Shuttle provides service from the airport in San Jose to downtown San Francisco for $69.

To drive to downtown San Jose from the airport, take Airport Boulevard east to Route 87 south. To get to San Francisco from the airport, take Airport Boulevard east to Route 87 south to I–280 north.

➤ **INFORMATION: Airport Express** (tel. 800/811–9773). **Bayporter Express** (tel. 415/467–1800). **East Bay Express Airporter** (tel. 510/547–0404). **Laurie's** (tel. 415/334–9000). **Marin Door to Door** (tel. 800/540–4815). **SamTrans** (tel. 800/660–4287). **SFO Airporter** (tel. 800/532–8405). **South & East Bay Airport Shuttle** (tel. 408/559–9477). **SuperShuttle** (tel. 415/558–8500 or 800/258–3826). **VIP Airport Shuttle** (tel. 408/885–1800 or 800/235–8847).

Bus Travel to and from San Francisco

Greyhound, the only long-distance bus company in San Francisco, operates buses to and from most major cities in the country.

➤ **BUS INFORMATION: Greyhound** (425 Mission St., tel. 415/495–1555 or 800/231–2222).

Bus Travel within San Francisco

The San Francisco Municipal Railway, or Muni, operates light-rail vehicles, the historic streetcar line along Market Street, trolley buses, and the world-famous cable cars. Light rail travels along Market Street to the Mission District and Noe Valley (J line), the Ingleside district (K line), and the Sunset District (L, M, and N lines). Muni provides 24-hour service to all areas of the city.

FARES
On buses and streetcars, the fare is $1. Exact change is required, and dollar bills are accepted in the fare boxes. For all Muni

vehicles other than cable cars, 90-minute transfers are issued free upon request at the time the fare is paid. Transfers are valid for a single ride in any direction.

A $6 pass good for unlimited travel all day on all routes can be purchased on the cable cars. Also, one-day ($6), three-day ($10), or seven-day ($15) Passports can be purchased at several outlets, including the cable car ticket booth at Powell and Market streets and the Visitors Information Center downstairs in Hallidie Plaza.

➤ **BUS INFORMATION: AC Transit** (tel. 510/839–2882) serves the East Bay. **Golden Gate Transit** (tel. 415/923–2000) serves Marin County. **San Francisco Municipal Railway System (Muni;** (tel. 415/673–6864, www.sfmuni.com) operates many routes within San Francisco.

Cable Cars

Don't miss the sensation of moving up and down some of San Francisco's steepest hills in a clanging cable car. As it pauses, jump aboard and wedge yourself into any available space. Then just hold on!

The fare (for one direction) is $2. You can buy tickets on board (exact change is preferred) or at the kiosks at the cable car turnarounds located at Hyde and Beach streets and Powell and Market streets.

Car Rental

In San Francisco, rates begin around $38 a day and $194 a week. The tax is 8¼%. There is also a charge for the vehicle license fee that varies with the value of the car, but you should expect to pay $1–$4 per day.

➤ **MAJOR AGENCIES: Alamo** (tel. 800/327–9633; 020/8759–6200 in the U.K.). **Avis** (tel. 800/331–1212; 800/879–2847 in Canada; 02/9353–9000 in Australia; 09/525–1982 in New

Zealand; 0870/606–0100 in the U.K.). **Budget** (tel. 800/527–0700; 0144/227–6266 in the U.K., through affiliate Europcar). **Dollar** (tel. 800/800–4000; 0124/622–0111 in the U.K., where it is known as Sixt Kenning; 02/9223–1444 in Australia). **Hertz** (tel. 800/654–3131; 800/263–0600 in Canada; 020/8897–2072 in the U.K.; 02/9669–2444 in Australia; 09/256–8690 in New Zealand). **National Car Rental** (tel. 800/227–7368; 0845/722–2525 in the U.K., where it is known as National Europe).

➤ **SPECIALTY CAR AGENCIES: SpecialtyRentals.com** (tel. 800/400–8412).

REQUIREMENTS & RESTRICTIONS

In California you must be 21 to rent a car, and rates may be higher if you're under 25. Some agencies will not rent to those between 21 and 24; check when you book. You'll pay extra for child seats (about $3 per day), which are compulsory for children under five. Children up to age six must be placed in booster seats. There is no extra charge for an additional driver. Non-U.S. residents must have a license whose text is in the Roman alphabet, though it need not be in English. An international license is recommended but not required.

Car Travel

Driving in San Francisco can be a challenge because of the hills, one-way streets, and traffic. Remember to curb your wheels when parking on hills (turn wheels away from the curb when facing uphill, toward the curb when facing downhill). Do use public transportation or cab it whenever possible.

PARKING

➤ **GARAGES: Ellis-O'Farrell Garage** (123 O'Farrell St., at Stockton St., tel. 415/986–4800). **Embarcadero Center Garage** (1–4 Embarcadero Center, between Battery and Drumm Sts., tel. 800/733–6318). **5th and Mission Garage** (833 Mission St., at 5th St., tel. 415/982–8522). **Opera Plaza Garage** (601 Van Ness Ave., at Turk St., tel. 415/771–4776). **Pier 39 Garage** (2550

Powell St., at the Embarcadero, tel. 415/705–5418). **Portsmouth Square Garage** (733 Kearny St., at Clay St., tel. 415/982–6353). **766 Vallejo Garage** (766 Vallejo St., at Powell St., tel. 415/989–4490). **Sutter-Stockton Garage** (444 Stockton St., at Sutter St., tel. 415/982–7275). **The Wharf Garage** (Fisherman's Wharf, 350 Beach St., at Taylor St., tel. 415/921–0226).

RULES OF THE ROAD

Always strap children under age five and weighing 40 pounds or less into approved child-safety seats; also children up to age six and weighing up to 60 pounds must be placed in booster seats designed to reduce seat belt injuries. Seat belts are required at all times; tickets can be given for failing to comply. Children must wear seat belts regardless of where they're seated.

Unless otherwise indicated, right turns are allowed at red lights after you've come to a full stop. Left turns onto adjoining one-way streets are allowed at red lights after you've come to a full stop. Drivers with a blood-alcohol level higher than 0.08 who are stopped by police are subject to arrest, and police can detain those with a level of 0.05 if they appear impaired. The state's drunk-driving laws are extremely tough. The licenses of violators may immediately be suspended, and offenders may have to spend the night in jail and pay hefty fines.

The speed limit on many rural highways is 70 mph. In the city, freeway speed limits are between 55 mph and 65 mph. In San Francisco, you need three people in a car to use commuter lanes.

Children in San Francisco

The City by the Bay is made for children—from the awesome hills to the ferries to the cable cars. Wherever you go in San Francisco, you're bound to find child-friendly activities.

SIGHTS & ATTRACTIONS

Most of San Francisco's major attractions, from Golden Gate Park to Fisherman's Wharf, are as fun for children as they are for adults. Places that are especially appealing to children are indicated by a rubber-duckie icon ( ) in the margin.

Consulates & Embassies

➤ **AUSTRALIA:** (625 Market St., Suite 200, San Francisco 94105, tel. 415/536–1970).

➤ **CANADA:** (550 S. Hope St., 9th floor, Los Angeles 90071–2627, tel. 213/346–2701).

➤ **NEW ZEALAND:** (12400 Wilshire Blvd., Suite 1150, Los Angeles 90025, tel. 310/207–1605; Box 330455, San Francisco 94133–0455, tel. 415/399–1255).

➤ **UNITED KINGDOM:** (One Sansome St., Suite 850, San Francisco 94104, tel. 415/981–3030).

Dining

The restaurants we list are the cream of the crop in each price category. Lunch hours are typically 11:30–2:30, and dinner service in most restaurants begins at 5:30 and ends at 10. Some restaurants stay open until midnight or later.

RESERVATIONS & DRESS

Reservations are always a good idea; we mention them only when they're essential or not accepted. Book as far ahead as you can, and reconfirm as soon as you arrive. We mention dress only when men are required to wear a jacket or a jacket and tie.

Emergencies

For police, fire, or ambulance, **dial 911.**

➤ **DOCTORS AND DENTISTS: California Pacific Center Physician Referral Service** (tel. 415/565–6333). **1-800/DENTIST** (tel. 800/336–8478). **St. Luke's Hospital Physician Referral Service** (tel. 415/821–3627). **San Francisco Dental Society Referral Service** (tel. 415/421–1435).

➤ **HOSPITALS: Two hospitals with 24-hour emergency rooms are San Francisco General Hospital** (1001 Potrero Ave., tel. 415/206–8111 emergency room; 415/206–8000 general information) and the **Medical Center at the University of California, San Francisco** (505 Parnassus Ave., at 2nd Ave., near Golden Gate Park, tel. 415/353–1037 emergency room; 415/476–1000 general information). **Physician Access Medical Center** (26 California St., tel. 415/397–2881) is a drop-in clinic in the Financial District, open weekdays 7:30–4.

➤ **24-HOUR PHARMACIES: Several Walgreens Drug Stores** have 24-hour pharmacies (498 Castro, at 18th St., tel. 415/861–3136; 25 Point Lobos, near 42nd Ave. and Geary St., tel. 415/386–0736; 3201 Divisadero St., at Lombard St., tel. 415/931–6417). The downtown Walgreens pharmacy (135 Powell St., near Market St., tel. 415/391–7222) is open weekdays 8–9, Saturday 9–5, and Sunday 10–5:30.

Gay & Lesbian Travel

San Francisco's reputation as a gay-friendly destination is well deserved. The Castro has long been thought of as ground zero for the gay community, but today gay men and lesbians have enclaves all over the city and in such surrounding communities as Oakland and Berkeley. Gay-owned shops and nightlife are sprinkled throughout the area as well. For details about the gay and lesbian scene, consult *Fodor's Gay Guide to the USA* (available in bookstores everywhere).

➤ **LOCAL RESOURCES:** *Bay Area Reporter* (395 9th St., San Francisco 94103, tel. 415/861–5019). **Billy DeFrank Lesbian & Gay Community Center** (175 Stockton Ave., San Jose 95126, tel. 408/293–2429). **The Lavender Youth Recreation & Information Center** (127 Collingwood St., San Francisco 94114, tel. 415/703–6150; 415/863–3636 for hot line). **Pacific Center Lesbian, Gay and Bisexual Switchboard** (2712 Telegraph Ave., Berkeley 94705, tel. 510/548–8283).

➤ **GAY- & LESBIAN-FRIENDLY TRAVEL AGENCIES: Different
Roads Travel** (8383 Wilshire Blvd., Suite 902, Beverly Hills, CA
90211, tel. 323/651–5557 or 800/429–8747, fax 323/651–3678).
Kennedy Travel (314 Jericho Turnpike, Floral Park, NY 11001,
tel. 516/352–4888 or 800/237–7433, fax 516/354–8849, www.
kennedytravel.com). **Now Voyager** (4406 18th St., San Francisco,
CA 94114, tel. 415/626–1169 or 800/255–6951, fax 415/626–
8626, www.nowvoyager.com). **Skylink Travel and Tour** (1006
Mendocino Ave., Santa Rosa, CA 95401, tel. 707/546–9888 or
800/225–5759, fax 707/546–9891, www.skylinktravel.com),
serving lesbian travelers.

Holidays

Major national holidays include New Year's Day (Jan. 1); Martin
Luther King Jr. Day (3rd Mon. in Jan.); President's Day (3rd Mon.
in Feb.); Memorial Day (last Mon. in May); Independence Day
(July 4); Labor Day (1st Mon. in Sept.); Thanksgiving Day (4th
Thurs. in Nov.); Christmas Eve and Christmas Day; and New
Year's Eve.

Lodging

The lodgings we list are the cream of the crop in each price
category. We always list the facilities that are available, but we
don't specify whether they cost extra. When pricing
accommodations, always ask what's included and what costs
extra. The hotel tax in San Francisco is 14%.

APARTMENT & VILLA RENTALS

If you want a home base that's roomy enough for a family and
comes with cooking facilities, **consider a furnished rental.**
These can save you money, especially if you're traveling with a
group. Home-exchange directories sometimes list rentals as
well as exchanges.

➤ **INTERNATIONAL AGENTS: Hideaways International** (767
Islington St., Portsmouth, NH 03801, tel. 603/430–4433 or 800/

843–4433, fax 603/430–4444, www.hideaways.com; membership $129). **Vacation Home Rentals Worldwide** (235 Kensington Ave., Norwood, NJ 07648, tel. 201/767–9393 or 800/633–3284, fax 201/767–5510, www.vhrww.com).

HOME EXCHANGES

If you would like to exchange your home for someone else's, **join a home-exchange organization,** which will send you its updated listings of available exchanges for a year and will include your own listing in at least one of them. It's up to you to make specific arrangements.

➤ **EXCHANGE CLUBS: HomeLink International** (Box 47747, Tampa, FL 33647, tel. 813/975–9825 or 800/638–3841, fax 813/ 910–8144, www.homelink.org; $98 per year). **Intervac U.S.** (Box 590504, San Francisco, CA 94159, tel. 800/756–4663, fax 415/ 435–7440, www.intervacus.com; $93 yearly fee includes one catalogue and on-line access).

HOSTELS

No matter what your age, you can save on lodging costs by staying at hostels. In some 5,000 locations in more than 70 countries around the world, Hostelling International (HI), the umbrella group for a number of national youth-hostel associations, offers single-sex, dorm-style beds and, at many hostels, rooms for couples and family accommodations. Membership in any HI national hostel association, open to travelers of all ages, allows you to stay in HI-affiliated hostels at member rates; one-year membership is about $25 for adults (C$26.75 in Canada, £9.30 in the United Kingdom, $30 in Australia, and $30 in New Zealand); hostels run about $10–$25 per night. Members have priority if the hostel is full; they're also eligible for discounts around the world, even on rail and bus travel in some countries.

➤ **ORGANIZATIONS: Australian Youth Hostel Association** (10 Mallett St., Camperdown, NSW 2050, Australia, tel. 02/

9565–1699, fax 02/9565–1325, www.yha.com.au). **Hostelling International—American Youth Hostels** (733 15th St. NW, Suite 840, Washington, DC 20005, tel. 202/783–6161, fax 202/ 783–6171, www.hiayh.org). **Hostelling International—Canada** (400–205 Catherine St., Ottawa, Ontario K2P 1C3, Canada, tel. 613/237–7884, fax 613/237–7868, www.hostellingintl.ca). **Youth Hostel Association of England and Wales** (Trevelyan House, 8 St. Stephen's Hill, St. Albans, Hertfordshire AL1 2DY, U.K., tel. 0870/8708808, fax 01727/844126, www.yha.org.uk). **Youth Hostels Association of New Zealand** (Box 436, Christchurch, New Zealand, tel. 03/379–9970, fax 03/365– 4476, www.yha.org.nz).

HOTELS

Most major hotel chains are represented in California. All hotels listed have private bath unless otherwise noted. Make any special needs known when you book your reservation. Guarantee your room with a credit card, or many hotels will automatically cancel your reservations if you don't show up by 4 PM. Many hotels, like airlines, overbook. It is best to **reconfirm your reservation directly with the hotel on the morning of your arrival date.**

➤ **TOLL-FREE NUMBERS: Best Western** (tel. 800/528– 1234, www.bestwestern.com). **Choice** (tel. 800/221–2222, www. hotelchoice.com). **Clarion** (tel. 800/252–7466, www.hotelchoice. com). **Colony** (tel. 800/777–1700, www.colony.com). **Comfort** (tel. 800/228–5150, www.comfortinn.com). **Days Inn** (tel. 800/ 325–2525, www.daysinn.com). **Doubletree and Red Lion Hotels** (tel. 800/222–8733, www.doubletree.com). **Embassy Suites** (tel. 800/362–2779, www.embassysuites.com). **Fairfield Inn** (tel. 800/228–2800, www.marriott.com). **Hilton** (tel. 800/ 445–8667, www.hilton.com). **Holiday Inn** (tel. 800/465–4329, www.basshotels.com). **Howard Johnson** (tel. 800/654–4656, www.hojo.com). **Hyatt Hotels & Resorts** (tel. 800/233– 1234, www.hyatt.com). **Inter-Continental** (tel. 800/327–0200, www.interconti.com). **La Quinta** (tel. 800/531–5900, www. laquinta.com). **Marriott** (tel. 800/228–9290, www.marriott. com). **Nikko Hotels International** (tel. 800/645–5687, www. nikkohotels.com). **Omni** (tel. 800/843–6664, www.omnihotels. com). **Quality Inn** (tel. 800/228–5151, www.qualityinn.com). **Radisson** (tel. 800/333–3333, www.radisson.com). **Ramada** (tel. 800/228–2828, www.ramada.com). **Renaissance Hotels & Resorts** (tel. 800/468–3571, www.renaissancehotels.com). **Ritz-Carlton** (tel. 800/241–3333, www.ritzcarlton.com). **Sheraton** (tel. 800/325–3535, www.starwood.com). **Sleep Inn** (tel. 800/753–3746, www.sleepinn.com). **Westin Hotels & Resorts** (tel. 800/228–3000, www.westin.com). **Wyndham Hotels & Resorts** (tel. 800/822–4200, www.wyndham.com).

Money Matters

Prices throughout this guide are given for adults. Reduced fees are almost always available for children, students, and senior citizens. For information on taxes, *see* Taxes.

CREDIT CARDS

Throughout this guide, the following abbreviations are used: **AE**, American Express; **D**, Discover; **DC**, Diners Club; **MC**, MasterCard; and **V**, Visa.

➤ **REPORTING LOST CARDS: To report lost or stolen credit cards: American Express** (tel. 800/327–2177); **Diners Club** (tel. 800/234–6377); **Discover** (tel. 800/347–2683); **MasterCard** (tel. 800/307–7309); and **Visa** (tel. 800/847–2911).

CURRENCY

The dollar is the basic unit of U.S. currency. It has 100 cents. Coins include the copper penny (1¢); the silvery nickel (5¢), dime (10¢), quarter (25¢), and half-dollar (50¢); and the golden $1 coin, replacing a now-rare silver dollar. Bills are denominated $1, $5, $10, $20, $50, and $100, all green and identical in size; designs vary.

Passports & Visas

When traveling internationally, carry your passport even if you don't need one (it's always the best form of ID) and **make two photocopies of the data page** (one for someone at home and another for you, carried separately from your passport). If you lose your passport, promptly call the nearest embassy or consulate and the local police.

Visitor visas are not necessary for Canadian citizens, or for citizens of Australia and the United Kingdom who are staying fewer than 90 days.

➤ **AUSTRALIAN CITIZENS: Australian Passport Office** (tel. 131–232). **U.S. Office of Australia Affairs** (MLC Centre, 19-29 Martin Pl., 59th floor, Sydney NSW 2000, Australia).

➤ **CANADIAN CITIZENS: Passport Office** (tel. 819/994–3500; 800/567–6868 in Canada).

➤ **NEW ZEALAND CITIZENS: New Zealand Passport Office** (tel. 04/494–0700 application procedures; 0800/225–050 in New Zealand for application-status updates). **U.S. Office of New Zealand Affairs** (29 Fitzherbert Terr., Thorndon, Wellington, New Zealand).

➤ **U.K. CITIZENS: London Passport Office** (tel. 0870/521–0410 for application procedures and emergency passports). **U.S. Embassy Visa Information Line** (tel. 01891/200–290). **U.S. Embassy Visa Branch** (5 Upper Grosvenor Sq., London W1A 1AE, U.K.); send a self-addressed, stamped envelope. **U.S. Consulate General** (Queen's House, Queen St., Belfast BTI 6EO, Northern Ireland).

Sightseeing Tours

In addition to bus and van tours of the city, most tour companies run excursions to various Bay Area and northern California destinations such as Marin County and the Wine Country, as well as farther-flung areas such as Monterey and

Yosemite. City tours generally last 3½ hours and cost $25–$30. Golden Gate Tours offers bay cruises ($38) as well as standard city bus tours. In addition to bay cruises, Gray Line offers city tours in motor coaches and motorized cable cars ($16–$32); Great Pacific Tours conducts the city tours (starting at $32).

➤ **INFORMATION: Golden Gate Tours** (tel. 415/788–5775). **Gray Line Tours** (tel. 415/558–9400, www.graylinesanfrancisco. com). **Great Pacific Tour** (tel. 415/626–4499, www.great pacifictour.com). **Tower Tours** (tel. 415/434–8687, www.towertours. com).

WALKING TOURS

The best way to see San Francisco is to hit the streets. Trevor Hailey leads a popular "Cruising the Castro" tour focusing on the history and development of the city's gay and lesbian community. Cookbook author Shirley Fong-Torres and her team lead a tour through Chinatown—"Chinatown with the Wok Wiz," with stops at Chinese herbal markets and art studios. The Chinese Culture Center leads a Chinatown heritage walk and a culinary walk for groups of four or more only. "Javawalk" explores San Francisco's historic ties to coffee while visiting a few of San Francisco's more than 300 cafés. "Victorian Home Walk" is a low-impact amble through some of the city's less traveled neighborhoods. Learn about the different styles of Victorian buildings while exploring Pacific Heights and Cow Hollow.

➤ **INFORMATION: San Francisco Convention and Visitors Bureau's Visitor Information Center** (tel. 415/974–6900, www.sfcvb.org). **City Guides** (tel. 415/557–4266). **"Chinatown with the Wok Wiz"** (tel. 415/981–8989, www.wokwiz.com). **Chinese Culture Center** (tel. 415/986–1822). **"Javawalk"** (tel. 415/673–9255, www.javawalk.com). **Trevor Hailey** (tel. 415/ 550–8110, www.webcastro.com/castrotour). **"Victorian Home Walk"** (tel. 415/252–9485, www.victorianwalk.com).

Smoking

In 1998 smoking became illegal in all the state's bars and restaurants. Though some bar owners have built outdoor patios or smoking rooms, others have refused to comply. There is typically not a lot of enforcement of this law, so take your cues from the locals. Hotels and motels are also decreasing their inventory of smoking rooms; inquire at the time you book your reservation if any are available. Additionally, there is a selective tax on cigarettes sold in California, and the prices can be as high as $4.50 per pack. You might want to bring a carton from home.

Taxes

Sales tax in San Francisco is 8½% and applies to all purchases except for prepackaged food; restaurant food is taxed. The hotel tax is 14%. Airlines include departure taxes in the price of the ticket.

Telephones

The 415 area code is used in San Francisco and Marin County. The area code south of San Francisco on the Peninsula is 650. San Jose and other South Bay cities use 408. Oakland and Berkeley use 510, and 925 covers the area east of the Oakland Hills, from Walnut Creek to Concord to Moraga. The area code in the Wine Country is 707.

OPERATOR & DIRECTORY ASSISTANCE

For operator assistance, dial "0." To obtain someone's phone number, call directory assistance, 555–1212 or occasionally 411 (free at public phones). To have the person you're calling foot the bill, phone collect; dial "0" instead of "1" before the 10-digit number.

INTERNATIONAL CALLS

Dial "011" + country code + city code + number. The country code for Australia is 61; New Zealand, 64; and the United

Kingdom, 44. The country code for Mexico is 52. To reach Canada, dial 1 + area code + number.

LONG-DISTANCE CALLS

Competitive long-distance carriers make calling within the United States relatively convenient and let you avoid hotel surcharges. By dialing an 800 number, you can get connected to the long-distance company of your choice.

▶ **LONG-DISTANCE CARRIERS: AT&T** (tel. 800/225–5288). **MCI** (tel. 800/888–8000). **Sprint** (tel. 800/366–2255).

PUBLIC PHONES

At pay phones, instructions are usually posted. Generally you insert coins in a slot (35¢ for local calls) and wait for a steady tone before dialing. When you call long-distance, the operator will tell you how much to insert; prepaid phone cards, widely available in various denominations, are easier. Call the number on the back, punch in the card's personal identification number when prompted, then dial your number.

Time

California is in the Pacific time zone. Pacific Daylight Time is in effect from early April through late October; Pacific Standard Time, the rest of the year. Clocks are set ahead one hour when Daylight Time begins, back one hour when it ends.

Tipping

At restaurants, a 15% tip is standard for waiters; up to 20% may be expected at more expensive establishments. The same goes for taxi drivers, bartenders, and hairdressers. Coat-check operators usually expect $1; bellhops and porters should get $1–$2 per bag; hotel maids in upscale hotels should get about $2 per day of your stay. A concierge typically receives a tip of $5–$10, with an additional gratuity for special services or favors.

On package tours, conductors and drivers usually get $1 per person from the group as a whole; check whether this has already been figured into your cost. For local sightseeing tours, you may individually tip the driver-guide 10%–15% if he or she has been helpful or informative. Ushers in theaters do not expect tips.

Train Travel to and from San Francisco

Amtrak trains travel to San Francisco and the Bay Area from different cities in California and the United States. The *Coast Starlight* travels north from Los Angeles to Seattle, passing the Bay Area along the way. Amtrak also has several inland routes between San Jose, Oakland, and Sacramento. The *California Zephyr* route travels from Chicago to the Bay Area. There is no Amtrak station in San Francisco. Instead, there is one Amtrak station in Emeryville, just over the Bay Bridge, and one in Oakland. A free shuttle operates between these two stations and the Ferry Building and CalTrain station in San Francisco.

Smoking is prohibited entirely on short-distance train trips. On long-distance train routes, smoking is allowed only in one section of the train. (The one exception is the long-distance *Coast Starlight*, where smoking is prohibited entirely.)

You can use Bay Area Rapid Transit (BART) trains to reach Oakland, Berkeley, Concord, Richmond, Fremont, Martinez, and Dublin/Pleasanton. Trains also travel south from San Francisco as far as Daly City and Colma. Fares range from $1.10 to $4.70; trains run until midnight.

CalTrain connects San Francisco to Palo Alto, San Jose, Santa Clara, and many smaller cities en route. In San Francisco, trains leave from the main depot at 4th and King streets, and a rail-side stop at 22nd and Pennsylvania streets. One-way fares run $1.25–$6.75. Trips last 1–1½ hours.

➤ **TRAIN INFORMATION: Amtrak** (tel. 800/872–7245). **Bay Area Rapid Transit** (tel. 650/992–2278). **CalTrain** (tel. 800/660–4287, www.caltrain.com).

Travel Agencies

A good travel agent puts your needs first. Look for an agency that has been in business at least five years, emphasizes customer service, and has someone on staff who specializes in your destination. In addition, **make sure the agency belongs to a professional trade organization.** The American Society of Travel Agents (ASTA), with more than 26,000 members in some 170 countries, is the largest and most influential in the field. Operating under the motto "Without a travel agent, you're on your own," it maintains and enforces a strict code of ethics and will step in to help mediate any agent-client disputes if necessary. ASTA also maintains a Web site that includes a directory of agents.

➤ **LOCAL AGENT REFERRALS: American Society of Travel Agents** (ASTA; tel. 800/965–2782 24-hr hot line, fax 703/739–7642, www.astanet.com). **Association of British Travel Agents** (68–71 Newman St., London W1T 3AH, U.K., tel. 020/7637–2444, fax 020/7637–0713, www.abtanet.com). **Association of Canadian Travel Agents** (130 Albert St., Ste. 1705, Ottawa, Ontario K1P 5G4, Canada, tel. 613/237–3657, fax 613/237–7502, www.acta.net). **Australian Federation of Travel Agents** (Level 3, 309 Pitt St., Sydney NSW 2000, Australia, tel. 02/9264–3299, fax 02/9264–1085, www.afta.com.au). **Travel Agents' Association of New Zealand** (Box 1888, Wellington 10033, New Zealand, tel. 04/499–0104, fax 04/499–0827, www.taanz.org.nz).

Visitor Information

The San Francisco Convention and Visitors Bureau can mail you brochures, maps, and festivals and events listings; or try the bureau's 24-hour fax-on-demand service (tel. 800/220–5747).

You can get information about the South Bay from the San Jose Visitor Information Center.

➤ **TOURIST INFORMATION: San Francisco Convention and Visitors Bureau's Visitor Information Center** (Box 429097, San Francisco 94142-9097, or lower level of Hallidie Plaza, tel. 415/391–2000 or 415/974–6900, www.sfvisitor.org).

Berkeley (2015 Center St., 1st floor, Berkeley 94704, tel. 800/847–4823). **Oakland** (475 14th St., Oakland 94612, tel. 510/839–9000, www.oaklandcvb.com). **San Jose** (333 W. San Carlos St., Suite 1000, San Jose 95110, tel. 408/295–9600 or 800/726–5673, www.sanjose.org).

Web Sites

Do check out the World Wide Web when planning your trip. You'll find everything from weather forecasts to virtual tours of famous cities. Be sure to **visit Fodors.com** (www.fodors.com), a complete travel-planning site. You can research prices and book plane tickets, hotel rooms, rental cars, vacation packages, and more. In addition, you can post your pressing questions in the Travel Talk section. Other planning tools include a currency converter and weather reports, and there are loads of links to travel resources.

GENERAL INFORMATION

The **California Division of Tourism** Web site (www.gocalif. ca.gov) has travel tips, events calendars, and other resources, and the site will link you—via the Regions icon—to the Web sites of city and regional tourism offices and attractions.

The Web site (www.sfvisitor.org) of the **San Francisco Convention and Visitors Bureau** has calendar listings and good maps.

When to Go

You can **visit San Francisco comfortably any time of year.** The climate here always feels Mediterranean and moderate—with a foggy, sometimes chilly twist. The temperature rarely drops lower than 40°F, and anything warmer than 80°F is considered a heat wave. Be prepared for rain in winter, especially December and January. Winds off the ocean can add to the chill factor, so pack warm clothing. North, east, and south of the city, summers are warmer. Shirtsleeves and thin cottons are usually fine for the Wine Country.

CLIMATE

The weather in San Francisco is remarkably consistent throughout the year. The average high is 63°F, while the average low is 51°F. Summer comes late in San Francisco, which sees its warmest days in September and October. Of the 20 inches of rain that falls on average each year, most of it comes from December to March.

➤ **FORECASTS: Weather Channel Connection** (tel. 900/932–8437), 95¢ per minute from a Touch-Tone phone.

SAN FRANCISCO

Jan.	55F	13C	May	66F	19C	Sept.	73F	23C
	41	5		48	9		51	11
Feb.	59F	15C	June	69F	21C	Oct.	69F	21C
	42	6		51	11		50	10
Mar.	60F	16C	July	69F	21C	Nov.	64F	18C
	44	7		51	11		44	7
Apr.	62F	17C	Aug.	69F	21C	Dec.	57F	14C
	46	8		53	12		42	6

INDEX

FODOR'S POCKET SAN FRANCISCO

EDITORS: Holly Hammond, Matt Hayes

Editorial Contributors: Denise M. Leto, Andy Moore, Sharon Silva, John Andrew Vlahides, Sharron S. Wood

Editorial Production: Taryn Luciani

Maps: David Lindroth, *cartographer*; Robert Blake, Rebecca Baer, *map editors*

Design: Fabrizio La Rocca, *creative director*; Tigist Getachew, *art director*; Melanie Marin, *photo editor*

Production/Manufacturing: Colleen Ziemba

Cover Photo (Golden Gate Bridge and viewing area): Martine Mouchy/ Stone

Fourteenth Edition

ISBN 0-676-90143-3

ISSN 1094-401X

IMPORTANT TIP

Although all prices, opening times, and other details in this book are based on information supplied to us at press time, changes occur all the time in the travel world, and Fodor's cannot accept responsibility for facts that become outdated or for inadvertent errors or omissions. So **always confirm information when it matters**, especially if you're making a detour to visit a specific place.

SPECIAL SALES

Fodor's Travel Publications are available at special discounts for bulk purchases for sales promotions or premiums. Special editions, including personalized covers, excerpts of existing guides, and corporate imprints, can be created in large quantities for special needs. For more information, contact your local bookseller or write to Special Markets, Fodor's Travel Publications, 280 Park Avenue, New York, NY 10017. Inquiries from Canada should be directed to your local Canadian bookseller or sent to Random House of Canada, Ltd., Marketing Department, 2775 Matheson Boulevard East, Mississauga, Ontario L4W 4P7. Inquiries from the United Kingdom should be sent to Fodor's Travel Publications, 20 Vauxhall Bridge Road, London SW1V 2SA, England.

PRINTED IN THE UNITED STATES OF AMERICA

10 9 8 7 6 5 4 3 2 1